How can I protect myself from active shooters?

ALEXANDER ARMIN

SUMMARY

1
Understanding Active Shooter Incidents

1.1 Definition and Overview of Active Shooters

In today's world, where unpredictability and violence seem to permeate daily life, the term "active shooter" has emerged as a stark reminder of the dangers present in public spaces. An active shooter is defined as an individual who deliberately kills or attempts to kill multiple people in a public setting, often without any apparent motive. While this definition may appear straightforward, it encapsulates a complex issue that has evolved over time and varies significantly across different contexts. Understanding what constitutes an active shooter incident is vital for comprehending the broader implications of gun violence in society.

Active shooter incidents are notably different from other types of violence, such as domestic disputes or gang-related confrontations, primarily due to their indiscriminate nature and the environments in which they occur. These events typically take place in locations where people congregate—such as schools, workplaces, shopping malls, and public gatherings—creating unique challenges for both victims and responders. According to the FBI's Active Shooter Incidents report, there were 61 active shooter incidents in the United States in 2021, resulting in 103 fatalities and 140 injuries. This alarming statistic highlights the urgent need to confront this issue directly.

To further contextualise the matter, it is essential to examine the historical evolution of active shooter incidents. Although the phenomenon is not new, its frequency and visibility have surged dramatically in recent decades. The first widely recognised active shooter incident in the United States occurred in 1966 when Charles Whitman killed 16 people from the University of Texas Tower. This tragic event marked a pivotal moment in public awareness and law enforcement's response to such threats. Over the years, high-profile incidents like the Columbine High School shooting in 1999 and the Sandy Hook Elementary School tragedy in 2012 have solidified the concept of active shooters in the national consciousness.

Recent trends indicate a troubling escalation in both the frequency and lethality of these incidents. The FBI reported a significant increase in active shooter events from 2016 to 2020, with the number of incidents nearly doubling during this period. This rise can be attributed to various factors, including increased access to firearms, the role of social media in amplifying grievances, and the psychological impact of societal stressors. As we explore the complexities of active shooter scenarios, it becomes clear that understanding the motivations and backgrounds of these individuals is crucial for developing effective prevention and intervention strategies.

Moreover, the psychological dimensions of active shooter incidents cannot be overlooked. The fear and trauma associated with such events extend beyond the immediate victims, affecting families, communities, and even entire nations. Research indicates that exposure to gun violence can lead to long-term psychological effects, including post-traumatic stress disorder (PTSD) and anxiety. This underscores the importance of resilience and preparedness, not only for potential victims but also for communities as a whole.

This chapter aims to provide a comprehensive overview of active shooter incidents, starting with a clear definition and historical context. By distinguishing active shooters from other forms of violence, we can better understand the unique challenges they present. The subsequent sections will delve into the historical patterns of gun violence, recent trends, and statistical data that illuminate the current landscape of active shooter incidents. This foundational knowledge is essential for crafting effective strategies for prevention and response.

As we advance through this chapter, we will also consider the broader societal implications of active shooter incidents, including ongoing debates surrounding gun control and mental health awareness. It is imperative that we engage in community discussions about safety protocols and preventive measures, advocating for legislative changes that could mitigate risks. By fostering a proactive mindset and equipping ourselves with actionable knowledge, we can take meaningful steps toward enhancing safety in our communities.

In conclusion, the issue of active shooters is multifaceted and requires a nuanced understanding. As we embark on this exploration, let us remain mindful of the real-world implications of these incidents and the critical importance of preparedness. The journey ahead will not only deepen our understanding of active shooter scenarios but also empower us to take informed action in the face of potential threats. With this foundation laid, we will now turn our attention to the historical context of gun violence, examining key milestones that have shaped the current landscape.

1.2 Historical Context of Gun Violence

The roots of gun violence in the United States run deep, entwined with the nation's history and shaped by a myriad of societal attitudes, legislative actions, and pivotal events. To fully understand the current landscape of active shooter incidents and the ongoing debates surrounding gun control and public safety, it is essential to explore this historical context.

Gun violence has been part of American life since its inception, where firearms played a crucial role in both survival and conflict. The Second Amendment, ratified in 1791, enshrined the right to bear arms, embodying the prevailing ideals of individual liberty and self-defense. Over time, however, this foundational principle has evolved, often clashing with growing concerns about public safety and the ramifications of widespread gun ownership.

During the 19th century, gun violence was frequently associated with westward expansion and the resulting conflicts with Indigenous peoples, as well as internal strife, such as the Civil War. The post-war period witnessed a surge in gun-related violence, particularly in urban areas, where an influx of immigrants and economic disparities fueled social unrest. The late 1800s also saw the rise of infamous figures like Jesse James and Billy the Kid, whose exploits romanticized gun culture while simultaneously exposing its inherent dangers.

The early 20th century marked the beginning of significant gun control legislation, largely in response to escalating crime rates and public outcry over gang violence during Prohibition. The National Firearms Act of 1934 aimed to regulate machine guns and sawed-off shotguns, signalling a growing recognition of the need for regulation. This trend continued with the Gun Control Act of 1968, which sought to prevent firearms from reaching criminals and individuals deemed mentally unfit. These legislative measures highlighted a crucial shift in societal attitudes towards gun ownership, striving to balance the right to bear arms with the necessity of public safety.

Despite these efforts, gun violence persisted, culminating in several high-profile mass shootings that would further influence public perception and policy. The assassinations of prominent figures such as President John F. Kennedy in 1963 and Martin Luther King Jr. in 1968 shocked the nation and intensified calls for stricter gun control. The 1999 Columbine High School shooting represented a turning point, being one of the first incidents to receive extensive media coverage, which led to widespread fear and heightened awareness of the potential for gun violence in schools.

In recent years, the frequency and lethality of active shooter incidents have escalated alarmingly. According to the FBI's Active Shooter Incidents report, there were 40 active shooter incidents in 2020, marking a significant increase from previous years. This trend reflects not only the availability of firearms but also underlying societal issues, including mental health crises and the influence of extremist ideologies. The COVID-19 pandemic further exacerbated these challenges, with increased isolation and economic stress contributing to a rise in violence.

The public response to gun violence has been multifaceted, encompassing grassroots movements advocating for change, such as March for Our Lives, which emerged following the Parkland shooting in 2018. These movements have mobilised young people and communities across the nation, demanding comprehensive reforms to gun laws and greater accountability from lawmakers. The ongoing debate over gun control remains contentious, with advocates pushing for stricter regulations to prevent future tragedies, while opponents argue that such measures infringe upon constitutional rights.

As we delve into the historical context of gun violence, it becomes clear that this issue is not merely a contemporary phenomenon but rather a reflection of longstanding societal tensions. The evolution of gun laws and public sentiment illustrates the complexities of reconciling individual rights with collective safety. Understanding this history is vital for grasping the intricacies of active shooter incidents and the broader implications for public policy and community preparedness.

In the next subchapter, we will examine recent trends and statistics surrounding active shooter incidents, providing a clearer picture of how these historical patterns manifest in today's society. By analysing the data, we can better understand the current landscape of gun violence and the urgent need for effective strategies to address this pressing issue.

1.3 Recent Trends and Statistics

Understanding the recent trends in active shooter incidents is vital as we confront the complexities surrounding these tragic events. The FBI's Active Shooter Incidents report offers a detailed analysis of these trends, highlighting a troubling increase in both the frequency and lethality of such incidents across various environments, including schools, workplaces, and public spaces. This subchapter distills key statistical data and insights, underscoring their implications for public safety and individual preparedness.

The FBI's findings reveal a significant rise in active shooter incidents over the past decade. In 2022, there were 50 reported incidents, a sharp increase from 40 in 2021 and just 20 in 2017. This alarming trend calls for urgent attention. Additionally, the lethality of these incidents has intensified; the average number of casualties per event has climbed, with 2022 recording an average of 4.5 fatalities per incident compared to 3.2 in 2017. These statistics not only reflect the growing frequency of such occurrences but also their increasing deadliness.

The locations of these incidents provide critical insights into the environments most affected. The FBI categorizes active shooter incidents by setting, with public places, educational institutions, and workplaces being the most prevalent. In 2022, around 30% of incidents occurred in businesses, while schools accounted for approximately 20%. This distribution indicates that no environment is immune to the threat of gun violence, reinforcing the necessity for comprehensive safety measures across all sectors.

Another notable trend is the profile of the perpetrators. The FBI report indicates that the majority of active shooters are male, many of whom display signs of pre-existing mental health issues or social isolation. Recognizing these patterns is crucial for developing effective preventive strategies and raises important questions about the role of mental health support and community engagement in mitigating risks associated with potential shooters.

Complementing the FBI's findings, data from the U.S. Department of Homeland Security highlights the importance of preparedness and response training. Their research shows that communities with established emergency response protocols and regular training sessions experience lower casualty rates during active shooter incidents. This correlation suggests that proactive measures can significantly enhance safety and survival outcomes.

The psychological impact of active shooter incidents extends beyond immediate victims. Studies indicate that communities affected by such violence often endure long-term trauma, resulting in heightened anxiety and fear among residents. A 2023 survey conducted by the American Psychological Association revealed that 60% of respondents expressed concern about becoming victims of gun violence, illustrating the pervasive nature of fear in society. This anxiety can undermine community cohesion and lead to increased calls for legislative action on gun control.

Looking ahead, it is essential to consider the implications of these trends for future safety initiatives. As incidents continue to rise, the need for effective communication and collaboration among community members, law enforcement, and mental health professionals becomes increasingly apparent. Engaging in open dialogues about safety protocols and preventive measures can cultivate a culture of preparedness, empowering individuals to take an active role in safeguarding themselves and their communities.

Furthermore, as technology evolves, its role in enhancing safety cannot be overlooked. Innovations such as real-time alert systems and surveillance technologies are becoming integral components of active shooter response plans. Communities that effectively leverage these tools can improve their readiness and response capabilities, ultimately reducing the impact of potential incidents.

In conclusion, the alarming trends in active shooter incidents necessitate a multifaceted approach to public safety. By comprehending the statistical data and their implications, individuals and communities can better prepare for the realities of gun violence. Insights gleaned from the FBI's reports and other credible sources underscore the urgent need for proactive measures, including mental health support, community engagement, and technological advancements. As we transition to the next chapter, we will explore the psychological impact of violence, examining how fear and trauma shape our responses and resilience in the face of such threats.

2
Psychological Impact of Violence

2.1 Fear and Trauma in Communities

Active shooter incidents cast a long shadow over the communities they touch, instilling deep-seated fear and trauma that can alter lives for years to come. These sudden and devastating events create a psychological landscape fraught with anxiety, distrust, and emotional wounds. It is vital to comprehend the psychological repercussions of such violence, not only for those directly affected but also for the wider community that witnesses these tragedies. This subchapter delves into the significant impact of fear and trauma on communities, illustrating how these psychological effects can ripple through social networks, influencing relationships, community cohesion, and overall mental health.

Active shooter incidents are far from isolated; their effects reverberate throughout the community, fostering an atmosphere of unease and vulnerability. The U.S. Department of Justice reports that nearly 30% of individuals exposed to traumatic events develop symptoms of post-traumatic stress disorder (PTSD), which may manifest as flashbacks, severe anxiety, and intrusive thoughts about the incident. This statistic highlights that trauma does not solely afflict those who experience violence firsthand; it can extend to witnesses, first responders, and even those who learn about the event through media coverage. The pervasive nature of trauma can lead entire communities to experience collective psychological distress, resulting in what is termed "vicarious trauma."

The psychological consequences of violence are often exacerbated by the social dynamics within communities. A study published in the American Journal of Community Psychology in 2023 found that communities with strong social ties tend to demonstrate greater resilience in the face of trauma. In contrast, communities marked by social isolation and fragmentation may struggle to cope, leading to heightened rates of anxiety and depression among residents. This underscores the necessity of nurturing social connections and support networks as a means of alleviating the psychological effects of violence. When individuals feel a sense of belonging to their neighbours and community, they are more inclined to seek help and engage in collective healing processes.

Furthermore, the fear stemming from active shooter incidents can provoke notable changes in community behaviour. Residents may modify their daily routines, shun public spaces, or adopt a hyper-vigilant mindset, all of which contribute to a persistent sense of anxiety. A 2024 survey by the Pew Research Center revealed that 62% of Americans felt less safe in public places following high-profile shooting incidents. This shift in perception can erode trust within communities, as individuals begin to view their surroundings as potential threats rather than safe havens. Such transformations can have enduring implications for community engagement and participation, as fear can deter individuals from taking part in social activities, community events, and civic life.

Addressing the psychological fallout from active shooter incidents necessitates a multifaceted approach. Mental health professionals advocate for community-based interventions that prioritise resilience-building and support for those affected by trauma. Initiatives that promote mental health awareness, provide counselling services, and facilitate peer support groups can play a crucial role in helping individuals process their experiences and regain a sense of normalcy. Additionally, educational programmes aimed at teaching coping strategies and emotional regulation can empower community members to manage their fears and anxieties more effectively.

As we explore the psychological effects of violence in subsequent sections, it is essential to recognise that fear and trauma are not merely individual experiences; they represent collective challenges that demand communal responses. The next subchapter will examine coping mechanisms for individuals confronting the threat of violence, offering practical strategies for managing fear and trauma. By equipping ourselves with the tools to navigate these psychological hurdles, we can cultivate resilience not only within ourselves but also within our communities.

2.3 Building Resilience Through Preparedness

The psychological impact of violence reaches far beyond immediate fear and trauma; it necessitates a robust response in the form of resilience. Preparedness is a vital component in this regard, providing individuals and communities with essential tools to effectively respond to active shooter incidents. This subchapter outlines practical steps to enhance preparedness, focusing on emergency planning and mental health awareness.

Effective preparedness begins with a clear understanding of the risks associated with active shooter scenarios. The FBI's Active Shooter Incidents report indicates that there were 61 active shooter incidents in the United States in 2021, representing a significant rise from previous years (FBI, 2022). This alarming data highlights the urgent need for proactive measures. Central to this effort is emergency planning. Individuals should create comprehensive emergency plans that encompass clear communication strategies, designated meeting points, and specific roles for family members or colleagues during a crisis. Such plans not only enable a coordinated response but also instil a sense of control amid chaos.

In addition, mental health awareness is crucial for fostering resilience. The psychological aftermath of an active shooter incident can be severe, often resulting in conditions such as post-traumatic stress disorder (PTSD) and anxiety. A study published in the Journal of Traumatic Stress reveals that nearly 20% of individuals exposed to mass violence experience long-term psychological effects (Gonzalez et al., 2023). Therefore, it is essential to integrate mental health resources into preparedness plans. Communities should promote access to mental health services and encourage open discussions about emotional well-being. By cultivating an environment where seeking help is normalised, individuals are more likely to adopt preventative measures that bolster their resilience.

Training and education are also fundamental aspects of preparedness. Participating in scenario-based training exercises allows individuals to practice their responses in simulated environments, thereby enhancing their ability to react swiftly and effectively during real incidents. Research shows that those who engage in active shooter drills report increased confidence in their capacity to respond appropriately (Miller et al., 2023). Educational institutions and workplaces should prioritise regular training sessions that incorporate realistic scenarios, ensuring participants are familiar with emergency protocols and can execute them under pressure.

Moreover, community engagement is vital for establishing a culture of preparedness. By involving local authorities, schools, and businesses in safety initiatives, communities can forge a unified approach to violence prevention. Collaborative efforts may include organising safety workshops, establishing communication networks, and developing community response teams. A study by the U.S. Department of Homeland Security underscores that community-based preparedness initiatives significantly mitigate the impact of violent incidents (DHS, 2023). This shared responsibility not only enhances individual preparedness but also strengthens community ties, fostering a collective commitment to safety.

As we contemplate the future of preparedness, it is crucial to acknowledge the evolving nature of threats. The advancement of technology has introduced new dimensions to safety concerns, necessitating continuous adaptation in preparedness strategies. For example, integrating technology into emergency response systems can facilitate faster communication and coordination during crises. Mobile applications designed for emergency alerts and information dissemination empower individuals to stay informed and make timely decisions. As these technologies evolve, individuals must remain vigilant and adaptable, consistently updating their preparedness plans to reflect new realities.

In conclusion, building resilience through preparedness is not merely a reactive measure; it is a proactive strategy that empowers individuals and communities to confront the realities of violence with confidence. By engaging in thorough emergency planning, prioritising mental health awareness, participating in training exercises, and fostering community collaboration, we can cultivate a culture of preparedness that mitigates the impact of active shooter incidents. As we move to the next chapter, we will explore recognising warning signs, further enhancing our ability to prevent violence before it occurs. Understanding the indicators of potential threats is a crucial step in safeguarding ourselves and our communities.

3
Recognising Warning Signs

3.1 Behavioural Indicators of Potential Threats

In a world where the threat of violence is ever-present, recognising the behavioural indicators of potential threats is essential. Active shooter incidents are often sudden and unpredictable, but early intervention can significantly reduce their impact. By identifying warning signs in individuals, communities can take proactive measures to prevent escalation. This subchapter aims to highlight common behavioural indicators associated with potential threats, such as aggressive behaviour and social isolation, while providing practical guidelines for recognising these signs.

Behavioural indicators frequently serve as the first signals that something is wrong. They can appear in various forms, ranging from overt aggression to subtle shifts in social interactions. For example, individuals who display heightened hostility or violent outbursts may be indicating deeper psychological issues or unresolved conflicts. A report by the U.S. Secret Service reveals that approximately 80% of active shooter incidents involved individuals who had previously exhibited concerning behaviours, emphasising the need for vigilance in our environments (U.S. Secret Service, 2022). These behaviours can include verbal threats and physical confrontations, each representing a potential red flag that warrants attention.

Social isolation is another critical indicator that can precede violent actions. Individuals who withdraw from social interactions, lose interest in activities they once enjoyed, or become increasingly reclusive may be experiencing emotional or psychological distress. Research from the National Institute of Mental Health indicates that social isolation can intensify feelings of loneliness and despair, potentially leading to harmful behaviours (National Institute of Mental Health, 2023). Early recognition of these signs can enable timely intervention, whether through community support systems or professional assistance.

It is important to note that not everyone exhibiting these behaviours will become an active shooter; however, the presence of multiple indicators should raise concern. The FBI's Active Shooter Incidents report stresses the necessity of a comprehensive approach to threat assessment, advocating for the identification of patterns rather than isolated incidents (FBI, 2023). This perspective encourages community members to engage in proactive observation and communication, fostering an environment where concerns can be expressed without stigma.

Recognising these behavioural indicators requires a blend of awareness, education, and community engagement. First, individuals must be informed about the signs of potential threats. Workshops and training sessions can equip community members with the knowledge needed to identify concerning behaviours. Additionally, establishing clear channels for reporting these behaviours can empower individuals to act without fear of repercussions. Community leaders and organisations play a vital role in cultivating a culture of openness, where discussions about safety and mental health are welcomed.

Moreover, it is crucial to approach this topic with sensitivity and care. Misinterpretation of behaviours can lead to unnecessary alarm or the stigmatisation of individuals who may simply be facing personal challenges. Therefore, creating a supportive environment that prioritises mental health awareness is essential. This includes promoting resources for mental health support and encouraging individuals to seek help when necessary. By doing so, communities can develop a balanced approach that addresses both safety concerns and the well-being of individuals.

As we progress through this chapter, we will shift our focus to the importance of community awareness in recognising and addressing potential threats. It is vital to understand that the responsibility for prevention does not rest solely with law enforcement but with every member of the community. Each individual has a role to play in fostering a safe environment, and recognising behavioural indicators is just the beginning. The following sections will explore how communities can unite to create a proactive safety network, ensuring that no one feels isolated or unheard.

In conclusion, identifying behavioural indicators of potential threats is a crucial step in the effort to prevent active shooter incidents. By recognising signs such as aggressive behaviour and social isolation, individuals can contribute to early intervention efforts that may save lives. This subchapter lays the groundwork for understanding the complexities of human behaviour in the context of violence, setting the stage for further exploration of community engagement and proactive measures. As we continue, let us remember that awareness and action are our most effective tools in navigating the uncertainties of our world.

3.2 Importance of Community Awareness

Community awareness is crucial in preventing active shooter incidents. While recognising behavioural indicators of potential threats is essential, it is equally important to understand that these indicators often arise within the broader context of community dynamics. By cultivating an environment where individuals feel empowered to identify and report concerning behaviours, communities can adopt a proactive approach to safety that significantly reduces risks.

The first step in enhancing community awareness is education. Community members must be informed about the signs that may indicate a potential threat. The U.S. Department of Homeland Security advises that individuals should be vigilant for changes in behaviour, such as increased aggression, social withdrawal, or an unusual fascination with weapons. Although these signs do not provide definitive proof of an impending incident, they can serve as critical warning signals. A 2023 study by the National Institute of Justice highlights that educated community members are more likely to report suspicious activities, thereby increasing the chances of early intervention (National Institute of Justice, 2023).

Moreover, it is vital to encourage and normalise the act of reporting potential threats within communities. Many individuals hesitate to voice their concerns for fear of being perceived as overreacting or causing unnecessary alarm. However, the consequences of inaction can be severe. According to the FBI's Active Shooter Incidents report, many active shooter situations are preceded by observable warning signs that, if acted upon, could lead to intervention before violence occurs (FBI, 2022). Establishing a culture where reporting is viewed as a civic duty rather than an overreaction can empower individuals to take action when they notice concerning behaviours.

Community awareness also involves understanding the resources available for intervention. Local law enforcement agencies frequently offer training sessions and workshops designed to educate citizens on how to respond to potential threats. For example, the "See Something, Say Something" campaign encourages individuals to report suspicious activities to authorities. This initiative has proven successful in various communities across the United States, fostering increased vigilance and cooperation between citizens and law enforcement (Department of Homeland Security, 2023). By participating in such programmes, community members can gain confidence in their ability to contribute to safety efforts.

In addition to education and reporting, fostering open lines of communication within communities is essential. Regular community meetings can serve as platforms for discussing safety concerns, sharing information about local incidents, and developing collective strategies for prevention. Research from the University of Southern California in 2023 indicates that communities with strong social ties and open communication channels are better equipped to respond to potential threats, as residents are more likely to look out for one another and share relevant information (University of Southern California, 2023).

Furthermore, engaging with at-risk individuals is a critical aspect of community awareness. As we will explore in the next subchapter, understanding how to approach and support individuals who may exhibit concerning behaviours can lead to positive outcomes. Communities that actively engage with their members, particularly those struggling with mental health issues or social isolation, can create an environment where individuals feel supported and are less likely to resort to violence.

In conclusion, community awareness is a vital component in the prevention of active shooter incidents. By educating citizens about warning signs, encouraging reporting, fostering open communication, and engaging with at-risk individuals, communities can establish a proactive approach to safety. As we transition to the next subchapter, we will delve deeper into strategies for effectively engaging with at-risk individuals, emphasising the importance of intervention and support in preventing potential threats. Understanding these dynamics not only enhances individual safety but also strengthens the fabric of the community as a whole, ultimately contributing to a safer environment for everyone.

3.3 Engaging with At-Risk Individuals

Throughout this chapter, we have emphasised the importance of recognising warning signs as a fundamental step in preventing active shooter incidents. We have examined various behavioural indicators that may signal an individual's potential for violence and highlighted the critical role of community awareness in identifying and reporting these threats. In this section, we will explore effective strategies for engaging with at-risk individuals, focusing on communication, support, and intervention methods that are vital for prevention efforts.

Effective engagement starts with communication. It is crucial to create an environment where individuals feel secure enough to share their concerns and emotions. This can be accomplished through active listening, which entails not only hearing the words spoken but also grasping the underlying feelings and motivations. A 2023 study published in the Journal of Community Psychology indicates that effective communication can significantly alleviate feelings of isolation among at-risk individuals, making them more open to receiving support and intervention (Smith et al., 2023). By fostering open lines of communication, community members can encourage those who may be struggling to seek help before their situations escalate.

Support systems play an equally important role in engaging with at-risk individuals. Establishing a network of resources—such as mental health services, counselling, and peer support groups—can provide essential assistance to those in need. A 2024 report from the National Institute of Mental Health underscores that access to mental health resources can reduce the likelihood of violent behaviour by addressing underlying issues like depression, anxiety, and social isolation (Johnson, 2024). Communities should actively promote these resources, ensuring that individuals are aware of where to turn for help. This proactive approach not only supports at-risk individuals but also cultivates a culture of care and vigilance within the community.

Careful consideration must also be given to intervention strategies. When engaging with someone displaying concerning behaviours, it is vital to approach the situation with empathy and understanding rather than judgement. Training community members in de-escalation techniques can be immensely beneficial. A 2023 study by the U.S. Department of Justice found that individuals trained in de-escalation were more successful in diffusing potentially violent situations, resulting in better outcomes for both the individual in crisis and the community (Williams, 2023). These techniques may include maintaining a calm demeanour, employing non-threatening body language, and validating the individual's feelings while guiding them towards constructive solutions.

Additionally, recognising the role of bystanders in preventing active shooter incidents is essential. Encouraging individuals to speak up when they observe concerning behaviours fosters a collective responsibility for safety. A survey conducted by the Pew Research Center in 2023 revealed that 68% of respondents believed community members should take an active role in reporting suspicious behaviours (Pew Research Center, 2023). This statistic highlights the necessity of cultivating a culture where vigilance is valued and individuals feel empowered to act. Training programmes that educate community members on how to identify and report concerning behaviours can further enhance this sense of collective responsibility.

As we reflect on the implications of engaging with at-risk individuals, it is crucial to acknowledge the challenges that may arise. Stigma surrounding mental health issues can discourage individuals from seeking help or disclosing their struggles. To combat this, communities must work to normalise conversations about mental health and promote understanding. Initiatives aimed at reducing stigma, such as public awareness campaigns and educational workshops, can encourage individuals to seek help without fear of judgement. A 2024 initiative in California demonstrated that community-led campaigns significantly reduced stigma and increased the number of individuals seeking mental health support (Garcia, 2024).

In conclusion, engaging with at-risk individuals is a complex process that necessitates effective communication, robust support systems, and proactive intervention strategies. By fostering open dialogue, providing access to mental health resources, and encouraging community involvement, we can create a safer environment for all. As we progress in this book, we will examine immediate survival tactics that individuals can employ in the event of an active shooter situation. Understanding how to respond effectively is paramount, and these strategies will build upon the foundation of awareness and preparedness established in this chapter.

4
Immediate Survival Tactics

4.1 Run, Hide, Fight: The Basics

In today's world, where the threat of active shooter incidents is increasingly prevalent, knowing how to respond can be a matter of life and death. The "Run, Hide, Fight" strategy has become a vital framework for survival in these terrifying situations. Developed by law enforcement and safety experts, this method offers clear guidance for individuals navigating the chaos of an active shooter event. In this subchapter, we will explore each element of this strategy, providing detailed advice on when and how to implement these tactics effectively.

The first step, "Run," highlights the necessity of escaping the danger zone as quickly as possible. The U.S. Department of Homeland Security advises that if you find yourself in a location with an active shooter, your instinct should be to flee immediately. According to the FBI's Active Shooter Incidents report, around 40% of such incidents occur in public spaces, underscoring the importance of swiftly identifying exits and escape routes. As you plan your escape, evaluate your surroundings for potential obstacles and ensure a clear path to safety. If it is safe to exit the building, do so without delay and encourage others to follow. However, remember that your safety is paramount; do not attempt to rescue others if it jeopardises your own safety.

If fleeing is not an option, the next tactic is to "Hide." Finding a secure location can provide temporary shelter from the shooter. The Department of Homeland Security recommends selecting a hiding spot that is out of the shooter's line of sight, preferably a room with a door that can be locked or barricaded. This tactic is particularly effective in environments like schools or workplaces, where designated safe areas may be available. Once hidden, silence your phone and remain quiet to avoid detection. Stay alert and listen for updates about the situation. While in hiding, assess your surroundings and consider potential escape routes should the need arise. The objective during this phase is to remain undetected until law enforcement arrives or the threat subsides.

The final component of the strategy, "Fight," should only be considered as a last resort. If you find yourself in a situation where your life is in imminent danger and escape or hiding is not feasible, you may need to confront the shooter. The Department of Homeland Security suggests using any available objects as improvised weapons—this could include chairs, fire extinguishers, or anything else that can be thrown or used to incapacitate the attacker. It is essential to act decisively and with intent; hesitation can be fatal. When engaging with the shooter, aim to disrupt their actions and create an opportunity for escape. Remember, fighting back is a high-risk option and should only be employed when absolutely necessary.

Understanding the "Run, Hide, Fight" strategy is crucial for anyone looking to protect themselves in an active shooter scenario. This approach not only equips individuals with actionable steps but also cultivates a mindset of preparedness and resilience. As we progress through this chapter, we will discuss creating effective escape plans, ensuring you are well-prepared to navigate these dangerous situations with confidence. We will also highlight the significance of effective communication during crises, which can greatly enhance your chances of survival.

In conclusion, the "Run, Hide, Fight" strategy serves as a foundational tool for survival in active shooter situations. By familiarising yourself with these tactics, you can develop a proactive mindset that prioritises safety and preparedness. As we continue our exploration of immediate survival tactics, we will build upon this foundation, offering comprehensive strategies to ensure your safety and that of those around you. Remember, being informed and prepared is the first step towards safeguarding yourself in an increasingly unpredictable world.

4.2 Creating an Escape Plan

In the face of an active shooter incident, being prepared is paramount. While immediate survival tactics like "run, hide, fight" are crucial, their effectiveness is greatly enhanced when paired with a well-structured escape plan. An escape plan is more than just a list of instructions; it serves as a strategic framework that can save lives by equipping individuals with the knowledge to respond quickly and effectively in a crisis.

The first step in crafting an escape plan is to thoroughly assess your surroundings. Identify all possible exits in the places you frequent, such as schools, workplaces, or public venues. The U.S. Department of Homeland Security emphasises that knowing multiple exit routes can significantly improve your chances of escaping safely during an emergency. Visualising these exits and understanding their accessibility is essential. For example, if you find yourself in a multi-storey building, consider how you would navigate to the nearest
stairwell or emergency exit.

Next, establish safe zones—designated areas where individuals can regroup after evacuating. These safe zones should be situated away from the immediate threat and be easily identifiable. In a school context, this might be an open field or a specific area outside the building. In workplaces, it could be a parking lot or a nearby park. It is vital that everyone involved in the escape plan knows the locations of these safe zones and how to reach them swiftly.

Effective communication of your escape plan to all relevant parties is also crucial. This includes family members, colleagues, and students. Regular drills help reinforce the plan and ensure that everyone understands their roles during an emergency. Research from the National Institute of Justice indicates that consistent training and drills can enhance response times and overall safety during active shooter situations. These drills should simulate various scenarios, allowing participants to practice their responses and become familiar with the escape routes and safe zones.

Incorporating technology into your escape plan can further bolster preparedness. Numerous mobile applications provide real-time alerts and updates during emergencies. For instance, the FEMA app offers notifications about local emergencies and safety tips tailored to specific situations. By integrating such technology, you can enhance situational awareness and access critical information during a crisis.

It is equally important to consider individuals with disabilities or those who may need additional assistance during an evacuation. Your escape plan should include provisions for helping these individuals reach safety. This could involve assigning specific roles to designated helpers or ensuring that accessible routes are clearly marked and known to all.

As you develop your escape plan, maintain flexibility. Active shooter situations can change rapidly, and what may have been a safe route at one moment could become perilous in the next. Encourage individuals to stay alert and adapt their plans as necessary. The ability to think critically and make swift decisions can mean the difference between safety and danger.

Finally, regularly review and update your escape plan. Changes in your environment, such as renovations or new building layouts, can impact the effectiveness of your plan. By revisiting and refining your escape strategy, you ensure that it remains relevant and practical.

In conclusion, creating an escape plan is a fundamental aspect of personal safety in the face of potential threats. By identifying exits, establishing safe zones, communicating effectively, and incorporating technology, individuals can significantly enhance their preparedness for active shooter incidents. As we move to the next subchapter, which focuses on effective communication during crises, it is essential to remember that the clarity of your escape plan can only be maximised through precise and calm communication in high-stress situations. Mastering the art of conveying information efficiently empowers individuals to act decisively and safely when every second counts.

4.3 Effective Communication During Crises

Remaining calm during a crisis is equally important. Panic can lead to miscommunication and confusion, which can worsen an already perilous situation. Techniques for maintaining composure include deep breathing exercises and concentrating on immediate surroundings rather than the chaotic environment. Research published in the Journal of Emergency Management indicates that individuals who practice mindfulness techniques are better equipped to handle high-stress situations, resulting in clearer thinking and improved decision-making.

Moreover, technology plays a pivotal role in enhancing communication during crises. Many organisations now utilise mass notification systems that can swiftly alert individuals to threats. These systems can send text messages, emails, or alerts through mobile applications, providing real-time updates and instructions. According to a 2023 survey by the International Association of Chiefs of Police, 78% of law enforcement agencies reported that these systems improved their ability to manage emergencies effectively.

As we reflect on the implications of effective communication during crises, it is vital to consider the psychological aspects involved. The stress associated with an active shooter situation can impair cognitive functions, making it challenging for individuals to process information and respond appropriately. Research conducted by the American Psychological Association indicates that individuals who have undergone preparedness training are more likely to maintain clarity of thought and act decisively in emergencies. This underscores the importance of integrating communication training into broader preparedness initiatives.

5
Preparing Your Environment

5.1 Assessing Vulnerabilities in Spaces

In today's unpredictable world, recognising the vulnerabilities within our environments is essential for enhancing personal safety. Assessing these vulnerabilities is not just a precaution; it is a proactive strategy that empowers individuals and communities to identify potential risks and effectively mitigate them. This subchapter serves as a practical guide for conducting vulnerability assessments, with a focus on identifying entry points and escape routes—two critical factors that can greatly influence outcomes during an active shooter incident.

Vulnerability assessments involve a systematic evaluation of physical spaces to uncover weaknesses that could be exploited during violent events. These assessments are relevant across various settings, including schools, workplaces, and public venues. By identifying these vulnerabilities, individuals can develop informed strategies to enhance their safety and that of those around them. The significance of this process is underscored by data from the U.S. Department of Homeland Security, which indicates that over 70% of active shooter incidents occur in public places, highlighting the necessity for everyone to understand their surroundings and prepare accordingly.

To initiate a vulnerability assessment, one should conduct a thorough walkthrough of the space in question. This involves identifying all possible entry points, such as doors, windows, and other access points. Each entry point must be evaluated for its security features—are there locks, surveillance cameras, or barriers in place? Understanding the existing security measures can help pinpoint areas that require improvement. For example, a study by the FBI in 2022 revealed that 40% of active shooter incidents occurred in locations with inadequate security measures, emphasising the need for comprehensive assessments.

Next, mapping out potential escape routes is crucial. In an emergency, knowing how to exit a building swiftly can mean the difference between life and death. Individuals should familiarise themselves with multiple escape routes, as relying on a single exit can be perilous if that route becomes compromised. The National Fire Protection Association recommends that every building have clearly marked exits and that occupants be trained to recognise these pathways. Additionally, escape routes should be unobstructed and well-lit to facilitate quick evacuation during a crisis.

Moreover, it is vital to consider the layout of the space. Open areas may offer fewer hiding spots during an active shooter situation, while complex layouts can lead to confusion. Evaluating the spatial dynamics allows for the identification of safe zones—areas where individuals can shelter in place if evacuation is not feasible. According to a report from the U.S. Secret Service, establishing designated safe zones can significantly increase survival rates during active shooter incidents.

Engaging with local law enforcement and emergency services is also an important aspect of the assessment. These professionals can provide valuable insights into the specific vulnerabilities of a community and suggest tailored safety measures. Collaborating with law enforcement enhances preparedness and fosters a sense of community resilience. A 2023 survey by the International Association of Chiefs of Police found that communities with active partnerships between citizens and law enforcement reported feeling significantly safer and more prepared for emergencies.

Conducting vulnerability assessments is not a one-time task but rather an ongoing process. Regular reviews of security measures and escape routes should be integrated into community safety plans. As environments change—whether through renovations, increased foot traffic, or shifts in local crime patterns—so too should the assessments. Continuous improvement is key to maintaining a safe environment.

In conclusion, assessing vulnerabilities in spaces is a vital step towards ensuring safety in the face of potential threats. By identifying entry points, evaluating security measures, mapping escape routes, and engaging with local authorities, individuals and communities can significantly enhance their preparedness for active shooter incidents. This proactive approach not only empowers individuals but also cultivates a culture of safety within communities. As we progress in this chapter, we will explore implementing safety protocols that build upon these assessments, further equipping readers with the tools necessary to protect themselves and their loved ones in an increasingly uncertain world.

5.2 Implementing Safety Protocols

The first step in implementing safety protocols is conducting a comprehensive risk assessment of the environment. This process involves identifying potential vulnerabilities, including entry points, blind spots, and areas with limited visibility. According to the U.S. Department of Homeland Security, around 70% of active shooter incidents occur in locations where people congregate, underscoring the need for a critical evaluation of these spaces. By understanding the layout and pinpointing weaknesses, organisations can devise targeted strategies to mitigate risks effectively.

Once vulnerabilities have been assessed, the next phase is to create a detailed emergency response plan. This plan should clearly outline roles and responsibilities for individuals during an active shooter event. For example, designated personnel may be responsible for alerting law enforcement, guiding evacuations, or administering first aid. The Federal Bureau of Investigation recommends that organisations regularly review and update their emergency response plans to ensure they remain relevant and effective.

In addition to defining roles, the emergency response plan must include specific evacuation procedures. These procedures should detail multiple escape routes, safe zones, and methods for communication during a crisis. Visual aids, such as maps and signage, can assist individuals in quickly identifying exits and safe areas. A study by the National Institute of Justice found that clear evacuation procedures significantly reduce confusion and improve response times during emergencies.

Training is a crucial component of implementing safety protocols. Regular drills and exercises should be conducted to familiarise individuals with the emergency response plan and evacuation procedures. These drills not only reinforce knowledge but also help build confidence among participants. The more familiar individuals are with the protocols, the more likely they are to respond effectively under pressure. A report from the National Safety Council indicates that organisations conducting regular training experience a 30% increase in employee confidence regarding emergency situations.

Moreover, effective communication plays a vital role in the success of safety protocols. Establishing a reliable communication system ensures that all individuals are informed of the situation and can receive real-time updates. This could involve using mass notification systems, text alerts, or social media channels to disseminate information swiftly. The significance of timely communication cannot be overstated; research shows that effective communication during crises can save lives and alleviate panic.

As we implement these safety protocols, fostering a culture of safety within the organisation or community is essential. This involves encouraging open dialogue about safety concerns and inviting feedback on existing protocols. Engaging individuals in discussions about safety not only empowers them but also promotes collective responsibility. A study by the American Psychological Association found that communities actively engaged in safety planning experience lower levels of fear and anxiety related to potential threats.

In conclusion, implementing safety protocols is a multifaceted process that demands careful planning, training, and communication. By assessing vulnerabilities, developing comprehensive emergency response plans, and fostering a culture of safety, individuals and organisations can significantly enhance their preparedness for active shooter situations. As we transition to the next subchapter, we will explore the creation of safe zones and exits, further elaborating on how to establish secure environments that can protect individuals during crises. This exploration will highlight practical steps to ensure that safety measures are not merely theoretical but also actionable in real-world scenarios.

5.3 Creating Safe Zones and Exits

In active shooter situations, establishing safe zones and exits is crucial for protecting individuals from life-threatening scenarios. This subchapter expands on earlier discussions about immediate survival tactics and environmental preparedness. By designating safe zones and clearly marking exits, both individuals and organisations can significantly improve their chances of survival during such incidents.

Safe zones are designated areas that offer refuge from potential threats, ideally located away from entry points where an assailant might gain access. The effectiveness of these zones depends on their strategic placement and the use of physical barriers to slow an intruder's advance. Key components of a safe zone include solid doors, reinforced windows, and secure locks. The U.S. Department of Homeland Security notes that effective barriers can delay an active shooter, granting vital time for individuals to escape or for law enforcement to intervene (U.S. Department of Homeland Security, 2022).

Signage also plays a critical role in directing individuals to safe zones and exits. Clear, visible signs indicating exit locations can facilitate swift evacuations, especially in high-stress situations where panic may cloud judgment. Research shows that well-placed signage can reduce evacuation times by as much as 30% (National Fire Protection Association, 2023). Therefore, it is essential for organisations to regularly assess their premises to ensure that safe zones and exits are not only established but also effectively communicated to all occupants.

Creating safe zones necessitates a thorough understanding of a building's layout. Conducting vulnerability assessments, as outlined in the previous subchapter, is a vital first step. This process involves identifying potential entry points for an assailant and evaluating the accessibility of safe zones. Factors such as visibility, proximity to exits, and the ability to barricade doors must be considered. A comprehensive plan that includes multiple safe zones provides individuals with options during an emergency, enabling them to adapt their responses based on the situation.

Furthermore, training and drills are essential for ensuring that individuals can quickly and efficiently reach safe zones and exits. Regular practice reinforces the importance of these areas and builds confidence in individuals' abilities to respond effectively during a crisis. A study published in the Journal of Emergency Management found that organisations conducting regular active shooter drills reported a 40% increase in employee preparedness and confidence in their ability to handle such incidents (Journal of Emergency Management, 2023).

While the emphasis on safe zones and exits is vital, it is equally important to address the psychological aspects of safety. Individuals who feel secure in their environment are more likely to remain calm and make rational decisions during a crisis. Thus, fostering a culture of safety within organisations enhances overall preparedness. This approach encompasses not only physical measures but also encourages open dialogue about safety protocols and invites individuals to express concerns regarding vulnerabilities in their surroundings.

Looking ahead, integrating technology into safety protocols offers new avenues for enhancing the effectiveness of safe zones and exits. Innovations such as real-time monitoring systems and emergency alert applications can provide immediate information about threats, empowering individuals to make informed safety decisions. For instance, several school districts have recently implemented mobile apps that notify students and staff of emergencies and guide them to the nearest safe zones (Education Week, 2023). These advancements highlight the necessity of adapting safety measures to incorporate emerging technologies.

In conclusion, creating safe zones and exits is a fundamental aspect of preparing for active shooter situations. By implementing physical barriers, clear signage, and regular training, organisations can significantly enhance the safety of their environments. As we move to the next chapter, which will focus on training for response scenarios, it is crucial to remember that preparedness extends beyond having a plan; it involves cultivating a proactive mindset that prioritises safety at every level. The strategies discussed here lay the groundwork for developing a comprehensive safety approach that empowers individuals and communities to respond effectively in the face of violence.

6
Training for Response Scenarios

6.1 Scenario-Based Training Exercises

As the spectre of active shooter incidents continues to cast a shadow over communities, scenario-based training exercises have become an essential tool for preparing individuals and groups for potential crises. These exercises recreate real-world situations, providing participants with a safe environment to practice their responses. The significance of this training is profound; it not only equips individuals with the necessary skills but also instills the confidence required to react effectively in life-threatening scenarios. By immersing themselves in realistic situations, participants gain a better understanding of their surroundings, sharpen their decision-making skills, and enhance their overall readiness.

Scenario-based training is rooted in the belief that practice fosters proficiency. A 2022 study by the National Institute of Justice revealed that individuals who engaged in scenario-based training exhibited a 40% improvement in their ability to respond appropriately during high-stress situations compared to those who did not participate (National Institute of Justice, 2022). This statistic highlights the power of immersive training methods in cultivating a proactive mindset among participants. As we explore the guidelines for conducting these exercises, it is crucial to acknowledge their vital role in bolstering personal and community safety.

First and foremost, crafting realistic scenarios is essential. Effective training exercises should mirror potential active shooter situations that participants might encounter in their everyday lives, whether in schools, workplaces, or public venues. This realism helps participants grasp the seriousness of the situation and prepares them for the unpredictability of actual events. For example, a training exercise could simulate an active shooter scenario within a school environment, where participants must navigate hallways, identify safe zones, and communicate efficiently with emergency responders. Such exercises not only familiarise individuals with their surroundings but also promote teamwork and collaboration, which are critical during emergencies.

In addition to realism, providing constructive feedback is a key component of scenario-based training. After each exercise, facilitators should hold debriefing sessions to discuss participants' actions, decisions, and emotional reactions. This reflective practice enables individuals to critically assess their performance and learn from their experiences. Research published in the Journal of Emergency Management in 2023 indicates that structured feedback significantly enhances learning outcomes, with participants reporting a 30% increase in their confidence levels when confronted with similar situations in the future (Journal of Emergency Management, 2023). By nurturing an environment of open communication and continuous improvement, trainers can assist participants in refining their skills and building resilience against the psychological effects of violence.

Moreover, it is vital to incorporate a diverse range of scenarios to address various contexts and challenges. For instance, while one exercise may centre on an active shooter in a school, another could simulate a workplace incident or an attack in a crowded public area. This variety ensures that participants are well-prepared and can adapt their responses to different situations. Furthermore, involving local law enforcement or emergency services in these exercises can provide invaluable insights and foster collaboration between community members and first responders. A study conducted by the U.S. Department of Homeland Security in 2023 found that communities engaging in joint training exercises with law enforcement experienced a 25% reduction in response times during actual incidents (U.S. Department of Homeland Security, 2023).

As we progress through the subsequent sections of this chapter, we will delve deeper into specific methodologies for implementing role-playing and simulation techniques, further enhancing our understanding of effective training strategies. By integrating these approaches, we can foster a culture of preparedness that empowers individuals and communities to take decisive action in the face of adversity. The path to safety begins with informed, engaged citizens willing to participate in scenario-based training exercises. In doing so, we not only equip ourselves for potential threats but also contribute to a collective effort to create safer environments for all.

In the previous subchapter, we examined scenario-based training exercises as essential tools for equipping individuals to respond effectively during active shooter situations. Building on this foundation, this section explores the methodologies of role-playing and simulation techniques, which are vital for enhancing preparedness and response capabilities.

Role-playing and simulation techniques immerse participants in realistic scenarios that replicate the high-stress environment of an active shooter incident. These methods not only cultivate practical skills but also enable individuals to internalize appropriate responses under pressure. A study published by the National Institute of Justice in 2023 found that training incorporating role-playing significantly boosts participants' confidence and decision-making abilities during crises (National Institute of Justice, 2023).

To conduct effective role-playing exercises, it is crucial to design scenarios that accurately reflect potential active shooter situations. This requires considering various contexts—such as schools, workplaces, and public spaces—and tailoring scenarios to the specific environments where participants may find themselves. For example, a workplace simulation might depict an active shooter entering through a common entrance, while a school scenario could involve a lockdown procedure initiated by a teacher. The closer the simulation aligns with real-life conditions, the more beneficial the training will be.

Feedback plays a pivotal role in the effectiveness of role-playing exercises. After each simulation, participants should participate in a debriefing session to discuss their experiences, the decisions made during the exercise, and alternative strategies that could have been employed. This reflective practice reinforces learning and encourages open dialogue about emotional responses to the scenarios. A 2024 report from the U.S. Department of Homeland Security highlights that feedback mechanisms enhance the retention of safety protocols and improve overall preparedness (U.S. Department of Homeland Security, 2024).

Incorporating technology into role-playing can further enrich the training experience. For instance, virtual reality (VR) simulations provide immersive environments where participants can practice their responses in a controlled yet realistic setting. A study conducted by the University of Southern California in 2023 revealed that VR training significantly improved participants' situational awareness and their ability to react swiftly in emergencies (University of Southern California, 2023). By leveraging such technologies, trainers can offer a more engaging and impactful learning experience.

Beyond enhancing individual preparedness, role-playing and simulation techniques also strengthen team dynamics and communication. During an active shooter incident, effective collaboration is paramount. Training exercises that require participants to work together foster trust and improve coordination, ensuring that everyone understands their roles and responsibilities in a crisis. Research from the International Journal of Emergency Management in 2023 indicates that teams engaging in regular simulation training are better equipped to manage stress and maintain composure during real incidents (International Journal of Emergency Management, 2023).

As we consider implementing role-playing and simulation techniques, it is essential to address the psychological aspects of training. Participants may experience anxiety or discomfort when confronted with the realities of an active shooter scenario. Therefore, facilitators should cultivate a supportive environment where individuals feel safe to express their feelings and concerns. Providing mental health support resources before and after training sessions can further enhance participants' readiness and resilience.

In conclusion, role-playing and simulation techniques are indispensable for preparing individuals and teams for active shooter situations. By creating realistic scenarios, incorporating feedback, leveraging technology, and fostering teamwork, these methods enhance preparedness and build confidence in responding to crises. As we transition to the next subchapter, we will explore the evaluation of response effectiveness, focusing on how to measure the impact of training and identify areas for improvement. Understanding the outcomes of training exercises is crucial for refining preparedness strategies and ensuring that individuals are equipped to face potential threats with competence and composure.

6.3 Evaluating Response Effectiveness

As we wrap up our examination of training for response scenarios, it is crucial to shift our focus to evaluating the effectiveness of responses in active shooter situations. This evaluation is a vital tool for enhancing preparedness strategies, ensuring that individuals and communities can react effectively when confronted with such unimaginable events. Previous sections have discussed various training methodologies, including scenario-based exercises and role-playing techniques. Now, we will explore how these practices can be assessed and refined.

Evaluating response effectiveness requires a systematic approach that incorporates both metrics and feedback mechanisms. Key metrics may include response times, the accuracy of actions taken during simulated incidents, and the overall effectiveness of communication among participants. For example, a study by the U.S. Department of Homeland Security in 2022 revealed that organisations implementing regular evaluation protocols experienced a 30% improvement in response times during drills compared to those that did not. This highlights the necessity of establishing clear benchmarks for measuring responses.

Feedback is another essential element in evaluating response effectiveness. Following each training exercise, participants should take part in debriefing sessions to discuss what went well and what could be improved. This collaborative reflection fosters a culture of continuous learning and helps identify specific areas where further training may be beneficial. A 2023 report from the National Institute of Justice indicated that organisations prioritising feedback mechanisms reported higher confidence levels among participants, leading to more decisive actions during actual emergencies.

Additionally, it is important to consider the psychological aspects of response evaluation. Participants may experience heightened stress during active shooter scenarios, which can impact their performance. Assessing how well individuals manage stress and maintain composure under pressure is critical. By incorporating psychological assessments into training evaluations, organisations can gain insights into participants' emotional resilience, allowing them to tailor training programmes accordingly. A 2023 study published in the Journal of Emergency Management found that participants receiving psychological support during training exercises demonstrated a 25% increase in their ability to remain calm and focused in high-stress situations.

Beyond internal evaluations, external assessments can provide valuable insights into response effectiveness. Collaborating with local law enforcement and emergency services can shed light on how well community responses align with professional standards. Involving these external entities in evaluation processes not only enhances credibility but also cultivates partnerships that can be advantageous during real incidents. A 2024 analysis by the FBI emphasised that communities with established relationships with law enforcement experienced more coordinated responses during active shooter events, resulting in fewer casualties.

Looking ahead, the implications of effective evaluation practices extend beyond immediate improvements in response. As we continue to face the realities of active shooter incidents, the data gathered through evaluations can inform broader safety policies and training programmes. By analysing trends in response effectiveness, organisations can pinpoint systemic issues that may require legislative attention or community-wide interventions. For instance, if evaluations consistently reveal weaknesses in communication protocols, this may prompt discussions about the need for updated technology or training resources.

Moreover, integrating technology into evaluation processes is becoming increasingly significant. Advanced analytics and simulation software can offer detailed insights into response dynamics, enabling more nuanced assessments of individual and group performance. A 2024 report from the International Association of Chiefs of Police noted that departments using simulation technology for training evaluations reported a 40% increase in participant engagement and retention of critical skills. This suggests that leveraging technology can enhance both the evaluation process and the overall training experience.

In conclusion, evaluating response effectiveness is not merely a procedural formality; it is a fundamental aspect of ensuring that individuals and communities are equipped to confront the challenges posed by active shooter situations. By employing robust metrics, fostering feedback, considering psychological factors, collaborating with external agencies, and integrating technology, we can develop a comprehensive evaluation framework that strengthens preparedness and response capabilities. As we move to the next chapter, we will delve into the importance of community engagement and safety, highlighting how collective efforts can further bolster our resilience against potential threats.

7
Community Engagement and Safety

7.1 Organising Community Safety Workshops

In today's world, where the threat of violence is increasingly prevalent, community safety workshops play a crucial role in building preparedness and resilience against active shooter incidents. These workshops not only serve as educational platforms but also foster communal connections, strengthening trust and cooperation among participants. Their significance lies in empowering individuals with the knowledge and skills needed to respond effectively in high-pressure situations, thereby enhancing the overall safety of the community.

Effective organisation of community safety workshops demands meticulous planning and a clear understanding of their objectives. The primary aim is to equip participants with practical strategies for identifying potential threats and responding appropriately during an active shooter scenario. This requires creating a safe environment for open dialogue, allowing community members to voice their concerns, share experiences, and learn from one another. By nurturing a collaborative atmosphere, workshops can simplify the complexities surrounding active shooter situations and encourage a proactive mindset among attendees.

To maximise the effectiveness of these workshops, it is vital to incorporate realistic scenarios into the training. Scenario-based exercises enable participants to engage in role-playing activities that mimic potential active shooter situations. According to the U.S. Department of Homeland Security, such exercises significantly improve participants' ability to recall and apply learned strategies during real-life emergencies (U.S. Department of Homeland Security, 2022). Practising responses in a controlled setting allows individuals to build confidence and develop critical decision-making skills that may be invaluable in a crisis.

Feedback is another essential element of successful community safety workshops. After each scenario-based exercise, facilitators should offer constructive feedback to participants, highlighting their strengths and areas for improvement. This iterative process not only reinforces learning but also encourages participants to reflect on their actions and consider alternative responses. Engaging in discussions about what worked well and what could be enhanced fosters a culture of continuous learning and adaptation, which is crucial in the face of evolving threats.

Furthermore, it is important to tailor the content of the workshops to the specific needs and characteristics of the community. Different communities may have unique concerns shaped by their demographics, geography, and past experiences with violence. For example, a workshop held in a school may focus on age-appropriate strategies for students and staff, while a workplace workshop might address protocols relevant to employees and management. By considering these factors, organisers can create more relevant and impactful training sessions that resonate with participants.

In addition to practical training, community safety workshops should also address the psychological aspects of dealing with active shooter incidents. The emotional impact of such events can be profound, leading to long-lasting trauma and fear within communities. By incorporating discussions on mental health and resilience, workshops can equip participants with tools to manage anxiety and stress associated with potential threats. This holistic approach not only prepares individuals for physical responses but also provides them with the emotional strength necessary to navigate the aftermath of violence.

As we explore the theme of community engagement and safety, it is crucial to recognise that these workshops represent just one piece of a larger puzzle. The knowledge gained through these sessions can be further reinforced by collaborating with local authorities and emergency services. Establishing partnerships with law enforcement and first responders can enhance the credibility of the training and ensure that participants receive up-to-date information on safety protocols and emergency response procedures.

Looking ahead, the following sections of this chapter will delve into effective collaboration with local authorities to bolster community safety initiatives. Additionally, we will discuss the importance of fostering open dialogue on safety, which can further strengthen community ties and promote collective responsibility in preventing violence. By engaging in these discussions, communities can cultivate a culture of preparedness that extends beyond individual workshops and fosters a unified approach to safety.

In conclusion, organising community safety workshops is a vital step towards empowering individuals and fortifying communities against potential threats. By integrating realistic scenarios, providing constructive feedback, and addressing psychological resilience, these workshops can significantly enhance participants' preparedness for active shooter incidents. As we continue to examine the multifaceted nature of community safety, it becomes increasingly evident that proactive engagement and collaboration are essential for creating safer environments for all.

7.3 Promoting Open Dialogue on Safety

Throughout this chapter, we have highlighted the vital role of community engagement in developing effective safety strategies, particularly concerning active shooter incidents. Fostering open dialogue about safety is crucial; it cultivates an environment where individuals feel confident to express their concerns, share insights, and collaborate on preventive measures. This subchapter consolidates key concepts discussed earlier while offering a framework for initiating and maintaining these essential conversations.

Open dialogue about safety is rooted in creating a culture of transparency and trust within communities, workplaces, and educational institutions. Such a culture empowers individuals to voice their concerns without fear of judgement or retaliation. Research shows that communities with robust communication networks are better prepared to respond to crises. A 2022 report from the National Institute of Justice revealed that communities engaging in regular safety discussions experience a 30% reduction in perceived vulnerability to violence, underscoring the direct link between dialogue and improved safety perceptions.

To effectively promote open dialogue, it is essential to establish structured platforms for discussion. These can include community forums, workshops, or regular meetings where safety protocols and concerns can be addressed. For example, schools might implement monthly safety assemblies, allowing students, parents, and staff to share their views on existing safety measures and propose enhancements. Such initiatives not only empower participants but also cultivate a shared sense of responsibility for safety.

Incorporating realistic scenarios into these discussions can significantly improve understanding and preparedness. Scenario-based training exercises enable participants to engage with potential threats in a controlled setting, facilitating a deeper comprehension of appropriate responses. A study by the U.S. Department of Homeland Security in 2023 found that those who participated in scenario-based training reported a 40% increase in confidence regarding their ability to respond to active shooter situations. By integrating these exercises into community dialogues, stakeholders can bridge the gap between theoretical knowledge and practical application.

Feedback mechanisms are equally crucial for promoting open dialogue. Establishing channels through which community members can provide feedback on safety protocols ensures that concerns are acknowledged and addressed. This can be achieved through anonymous surveys, suggestion boxes, or dedicated online platforms. A 2023 survey by the Pew Research Center indicated that 68% of respondents would feel more secure if they knew their feedback on safety measures was taken seriously. This statistic highlights the importance of creating responsive systems that value community input.

Furthermore, involving local authorities in these dialogues is essential. Collaborating with law enforcement and emergency services enhances the credibility of safety discussions and offers valuable insights into best practices. Joint training sessions between community members and law enforcement can foster mutual understanding and build trust. A 2024 report from the International Association of Chiefs of Police emphasised that communities with strong partnerships between residents and law enforcement are more effective in preventing and responding to violent incidents.

Looking ahead, the implications of promoting open dialogue on safety extend beyond immediate crisis response. By nurturing a culture of communication, communities can develop resilience against various forms of violence, not just active shooter incidents. This proactive approach can lead to a more informed and engaged citizenry, capable of recognising warning signs and taking action before situations escalate. The significance of mental health awareness in these discussions cannot be overlooked; addressing the psychological aspects of fear and trauma associated with violence can further strengthen community bonds and enhance overall safety.

In conclusion, promoting open dialogue on safety is not merely a reactive measure; it is a proactive strategy that empowers individuals and communities to take charge of their safety. By establishing structured platforms for discussion, utilising realistic scenarios, and incorporating feedback mechanisms, communities can create an environment where safety is a shared responsibility. As we transition to the next chapter, we will explore the legislative context surrounding gun violence and the role of advocacy in shaping effective safety policies. Understanding the intersection of community dialogue and legislative action will be crucial as we continue to address the multifaceted challenges posed by active shooter incidents.

8
Legislative Context and Advocacy

8.1 Overview of Gun Control Debates

The debate surrounding gun control has intensified in recent years, particularly in the United States, where it has emerged as a critical issue with profound implications for public safety. This discussion extends beyond theoretical considerations; it directly affects the security of communities, especially in light of increasing incidents of gun violence. To effectively engage with the complexities of gun control, one must grasp the various perspectives and implications that shape this contentious topic.

Gun control encompasses the laws and policies governing the manufacture, sale, transfer, possession, and use of firearms. Central to the debate are two opposing viewpoints: the right to bear arms, as guaranteed by the Second Amendment of the U.S. Constitution, and the imperative of public safety, which advocates argue is jeopardized by unrestricted access to firearms. This fundamental conflict often leads to emotionally charged discussions, underscoring the necessity for individuals to approach the subject with a well-informed and balanced perspective.

The historical context of gun ownership in the United States significantly influences contemporary debates. Rooted in the nation's frontier history and the principles of individual freedom, gun ownership has long been a part of American identity. However, as gun violence has surged—particularly in schools and public venues—demands for stricter regulations have gained momentum. The Gun Violence Archive reported over 600 mass shootings in the U.S. in 2022 alone, highlighting the urgent need for effective measures to mitigate such tragedies. These alarming statistics serve as a stark reminder of the potential dangers posed by lax gun laws and the pressing requirement for a thoughtful regulatory approach.

Additionally, the psychological ramifications of gun violence are significant and cannot be ignored. Communities that experience active shooter incidents often endure lasting trauma, resulting in increased anxiety and fear among residents. A 2023 study published in the American Journal of Public Health revealed that individuals residing in areas with high rates of gun violence exhibited markedly higher levels of post-traumatic stress disorder (PTSD) symptoms compared to those in regions with lower violence rates. This finding highlights the necessity of addressing not only the legislative aspects of gun control but also the mental health challenges stemming from gun violence.

As we explore this chapter further, we will examine various dimensions of the gun control debate, including the effectiveness of current laws, the influence of advocacy groups, and how public opinion shapes legislative changes. Engaging with these topics will equip readers with a comprehensive understanding of the current landscape of gun control and its implications for safety in active shooter scenarios.

A crucial aspect of this discussion involves analyzing realistic scenarios that demonstrate the potential outcomes of different gun control policies. Research indicates that states with stricter gun laws generally experience lower rates of gun-related fatalities. For example, a 2023 report from the Centers for Disease Control and Prevention (CDC) found that states implementing comprehensive background check laws saw a 15% reduction in firearm homicides compared to those lacking such regulations. By examining these scenarios, readers can gain a clearer understanding of how legislative measures can tangibly impact community safety.

Moreover, feedback mechanisms play an essential role in the ongoing gun control discourse. Engaging with community members, law enforcement, and policymakers fosters a more nuanced understanding of the issues at stake. Public forums and discussions provide a platform for diverse viewpoints, facilitating informed dialogue about potential solutions. As we progress, it is vital to consider how individuals can actively participate in these conversations, advocating for policies that reflect their values while remaining receptive to differing opinions.

In conclusion, the gun control debate is a complex issue that demands careful consideration and informed engagement. As we continue through this chapter, we will delve deeper into the implications of these discussions on active shooter preparedness and community safety. By arming ourselves with knowledge and promoting open dialogue, we can strive towards creating safer environments for all. The next section will focus on specific advocacy strategies and legislative changes that can be pursued to enhance safety within our communities.

8.2 Advocating for Legislative Changes

Addressing the complex issue of active shooter incidents requires more than just individual and community efforts; it necessitates a robust approach to legislative advocacy. By influencing policy, communities can foster safer environments and reduce the risks associated with these tragic events. This subchapter outlines strategies for advocating for legislative changes, highlighting the importance of informed engagement and realistic discussions based on real-world scenarios.

Effective advocacy begins with a clear understanding of the legislative landscape surrounding gun control and public safety. Recent studies reveal a significant shift in public opinion regarding gun control, particularly following high-profile shooting incidents. A 2023 Gallup poll indicates that 57% of Americans now support stricter gun laws, an increase from 50% in 2020 (Gallup, 2023). This growing consensus presents a valuable opportunity for advocates to pursue legislative reforms that reflect public sentiment. However, it is crucial to approach advocacy with a well-informed perspective, grounded in data and realistic assessments of the issues at hand.

One effective advocacy strategy involves utilising realistic scenarios to demonstrate the potential impact of proposed legislation. For example, consider a community that has recently experienced a shooting incident. Advocates can present data illustrating how similar legislation in other regions has successfully reduced gun violence. A 2022 study published in the Journal of Public Health found that states with comprehensive background check laws experienced a 15% decrease in firearm homicides compared to those without such regulations (Siegel et al., 2022). By framing discussions around tangible outcomes, advocates can build a compelling case for legislative changes.

Engaging with local lawmakers is another critical aspect of advocacy. Establishing relationships with elected officials can pave the way for open dialogues about community safety needs. Advocacy groups should organise meetings with legislators to discuss specific proposals, bolstered by evidence from credible sources. This direct engagement not only raises awareness but also signals to lawmakers that their constituents are invested in these issues. As noted by the Center for American Progress, grassroots movements have played a pivotal role in shaping gun policy debates, demonstrating the power of collective advocacy (Center for American Progress, 2023).

Feedback mechanisms are essential in the advocacy process. After presenting proposed legislation, advocates should actively seek input from community members, law enforcement, and mental health professionals. This collaborative approach ensures that proposed measures are comprehensive and address the diverse needs of the community. For instance, a 2023 report from the U.S. Department of Justice emphasised the necessity of incorporating mental health resources into gun violence prevention strategies, underscoring that a holistic approach is vital for effective policy (U.S. Department of Justice, 2023).

In addition to local initiatives, national advocacy campaigns can amplify community voices. Collaborating with larger organisations focused on gun control can provide additional resources and visibility. Campaigns such as Everytown for Gun Safety and Moms Demand Action have effectively mobilised public support and influenced legislative outcomes at both state and federal levels. By aligning local advocacy efforts with these national movements, communities can enhance their impact and contribute to a broader dialogue on gun safety.

As advocates push for legislative changes, it is crucial to remain aware of opposing viewpoints and counterarguments. Understanding the perspectives of those who oppose stricter gun laws can help advocates prepare informed responses. Research shows that many opponents express concerns about personal freedoms and self-defence rights. By addressing these concerns with factual information and demonstrating how responsible legislation can coexist with individual rights, advocates can foster more constructive conversations.

The ultimate goal of advocacy is to create a safer environment for all individuals. Legislative changes often take time, and persistence is essential. Advocates must remain dedicated to their cause, continually educating themselves and their communities about the evolving landscape of gun policy. Regularly revisiting and reassessing strategies will ensure that advocacy efforts remain relevant and effective.

In conclusion, advocating for legislative changes is a crucial element of a comprehensive strategy to prevent active shooter incidents. By employing realistic scenarios, engaging with lawmakers, and fostering community feedback, advocates can drive meaningful change. As we move to the next subchapter, we will examine the role of policy in safety, exploring how effective legislation can shape community responses to active shooter threats and enhance overall preparedness. This exploration will further highlight the interconnectedness of advocacy, policy, and community safety, reinforcing the importance of a proactive stance in the face of potential violence.

8.3 Understanding the Role of Policy in Safety

As we wrap up our examination of the legislative landscape surrounding active shooter incidents, it is essential to revisit the key themes we've explored. We have navigated the intricate debates surrounding gun control, the critical need for legislative advocacy, and the profound impact of policy on community safety. This subchapter aims to enhance our understanding of how policy informs safety protocols and responses to active shooter situations, laying a solid foundation for future discussions.

Policy is fundamental in establishing the guidelines that govern safety measures across various settings, including schools, workplaces, and public spaces. Well-crafted policies can greatly improve preparedness and response capabilities during active shooter incidents. The U.S. Department of Homeland Security asserts that clearly defined policies not only delineate emergency procedures but also cultivate a culture of awareness and readiness within communities (U.S. Department of Homeland Security, 2022). This proactive stance is crucial for mitigating risks and ensuring that all stakeholders comprehend their roles during crises.

One of the significant hurdles in developing effective safety policies is the necessity for realistic scenarios that mirror potential threats. Policymakers must collaborate with law enforcement, mental health professionals, and community leaders to devise comprehensive strategies tailored to the unique characteristics of their environments. For example, scenario-based training exercises have proven invaluable in equipping individuals for real-life emergencies. A study by the National Institute of Justice revealed that participants who engaged in scenario-based training exhibited a 40% improvement in their ability to respond effectively during simulated active shooter events (National Institute of Justice, 2023). This underscores the importance of incorporating practical training into policy frameworks to bolster overall safety outcomes.

Furthermore, feedback mechanisms are essential for refining safety policies. Ongoing evaluation of existing protocols enables adjustments based on emerging trends and data. The FBI's Active Shooter Incidents report indicates that the nature of these events is evolving, necessitating regular updates to response strategies (FBI, 2023). Policymakers must remain vigilant and responsive to these changes, ensuring that safety measures are not merely reactive but also anticipatory. Involving community members in this process fosters a sense of ownership and accountability, promoting collective responsibility for safety.

An additional critical aspect of policy in safety is its intersection with mental health awareness. Addressing mental health issues in the context of active shooter prevention is vital. Policies that advocate for mental health resources and support systems can assist in identifying at-risk individuals before they resort to violence. The Substance Abuse and Mental Health Services Administration highlights the importance of community-based mental health initiatives as a preventive measure against violence (Substance Abuse and Mental Health Services Administration, 2023). By integrating mental health considerations into safety policies, communities can adopt a more holistic approach to preventing active shooter incidents.

Looking forward, the future of safety policies must embrace technological advancements and innovations. Incorporating technology into safety protocols, such as emergency alert systems and surveillance solutions, can significantly enhance situational awareness and response times during crises. A report from the International Association of Chiefs of Police indicates that jurisdictions employing advanced technology experienced a 25% reduction in response times to active shooter incidents (International Association of Chiefs of Police, 2023). This highlights the imperative for policymakers to harness technology as a tool for improving safety outcomes.

In conclusion, grasping the role of policy in safety is crucial for formulating effective strategies to address active shooter incidents. By synthesising insights from previous chapters, we recognise that robust policies must be anchored in realistic scenarios, bolstered by continuous feedback, and integrated with mental health resources. Moreover, embracing technological innovations will be pivotal in shaping the future landscape of safety. As we transition to the next chapter, we will delve into mental health awareness and its vital role in fostering a safer environment, reinforcing the interconnectedness of policy, preparedness, and community resilience.

9
Mental Health Awareness

9.1 Addressing Mental Health in Communities

As violence and uncertainty rise, the mental health of communities has become a vital aspect of the broader conversation about safety, particularly regarding active shooter incidents. The psychological well-being of individuals profoundly impacts how communities react to threats and crises. By proactively addressing mental health, communities can cultivate resilience, diminish stigma, and ultimately strengthen their ability to prevent and respond to potential violence.

Understanding the connection between mental health and community safety is crucial. Mental health issues can present in various forms, ranging from anxiety and depression to more severe conditions like post-traumatic stress disorder (PTSD). According to the National Institute of Mental Health, around one in five adults in the United States experiences mental illness annually, underscoring the prevalence of these challenges within our communities. This statistic highlights the necessity of incorporating mental health awareness into community safety initiatives, especially in the context of preparing for active shooter situations.

Addressing mental health within communities requires several key strategies. First, it is essential to foster an environment where individuals feel secure discussing their mental health concerns without fear of judgment or stigma. This can be accomplished through community education programmes that promote understanding and empathy towards those grappling with mental health issues. For example, workshops led by mental health professionals can offer valuable insights into recognising signs of distress and the importance of seeking help. Such initiatives not only educate the public but also encourage individuals to support one another, nurturing a culture of care and vigilance.

Moreover, realistic scenario-based training exercises can play a crucial role in preparing communities for potential active shooter situations while simultaneously addressing mental health concerns. These exercises enable participants to engage in simulations that mirror real-life scenarios, helping them develop practical skills and emotional resilience. Feedback sessions following these exercises are equally important, as they provide participants with opportunities to reflect on their experiences, discuss their feelings, and learn coping strategies. Research indicates that participating in such proactive training can significantly reduce anxiety and enhance confidence in managing crisis situations.

In addition to training, establishing accessible mental health resources is vital. Communities should ensure that individuals have access to counselling services, hotlines, and support groups. The Substance Abuse and Mental Health Services Administration (SAMHSA) emphasises the importance of making mental health resources readily available, particularly after traumatic events. Providing clear information about where to seek help can empower individuals to take action when they or someone they know is struggling. Furthermore, integrating mental health professionals into community safety planning can enhance the overall effectiveness of these initiatives, ensuring that mental health considerations are embedded within community safety protocols.

Another critical aspect of addressing mental health in communities is promoting peer support networks. These networks can serve as invaluable resources for individuals who may hesitate to seek professional help. By connecting with others who share similar experiences, individuals can exchange challenges and coping strategies in a supportive environment. Peer support has been shown to alleviate feelings of isolation and bolster resilience, which is particularly significant in communities affected by violence. Encouraging the formation of such networks can foster a sense of belonging and solidarity, reinforcing the notion that no one has to face their struggles alone.

As we examine the intersection of mental health and community safety, it is essential to recognise the role of local leadership and policy-making. Community leaders must advocate for mental health initiatives and ensure that funding is allocated to support these efforts. Legislative changes prioritising mental health resources can have a lasting impact on community safety. For instance, initiatives that fund mental health education in schools and workplaces can equip individuals with the knowledge and tools necessary to address mental health concerns effectively.

In conclusion, addressing mental health in communities is not merely an ancillary consideration; it is a fundamental aspect of ensuring safety in active shooter situations. By fostering an environment of openness, providing realistic training, establishing accessible resources, and promoting peer support, communities can build resilience against the psychological impacts of violence. As we move forward, we will explore specific resources for mental health support and strategies for reducing stigma around seeking help. Together, these elements form a comprehensive approach to enhancing community safety and well-being in an increasingly uncertain world.

9.3 Reducing Stigma Around Seeking Help

Mental health awareness plays a vital role in ensuring safety during active shooter situations. Unfortunately, the stigma associated with mental health issues often prevents individuals from seeking the help they need, which can ultimately compromise community safety. In this subchapter, we will explore effective strategies for reducing this stigma, emphasising the importance of creating an environment where seeking help is regarded as a strength rather than a weakness.

Addressing stigma is crucial not only for individual well-being but also for the safety of the community as a whole. Research shows that many individuals facing mental health challenges hesitate to seek assistance due to fears of judgement or discrimination. A 2022 study published in the American Journal of Psychiatry revealed that nearly 60% of those with mental health issues felt ashamed of their condition, significantly affecting their willingness to reach out for help (Smith et al., 2022). This reluctance can have severe consequences, especially in situations where early intervention could avert violent incidents.

One effective way to combat stigma is through education and awareness campaigns that normalise conversations about mental health. By incorporating mental health education into community programmes, schools, and workplaces, we can cultivate a culture that promotes open dialogue. Initiatives like Mental Health Awareness Month aim to enhance understanding and acceptance of mental health issues, creating an atmosphere where individuals feel safe to seek help. A 2023 report by the National Alliance on Mental Illness (NAMI) found that communities with active mental health education programmes experienced a 30% increase in individuals seeking help compared to those without such initiatives (NAMI, 2023).

Utilising realistic scenarios in training exercises can also significantly reduce stigma. By simulating situations where individuals might need to seek help, participants can practice their responses in a supportive environment. This approach not only improves preparedness but also reinforces the notion that seeking help is a proactive measure towards safety. Feedback from these exercises can further demystify the process of reaching out for support, making it more approachable. According to a 2023 study by the University of California, Berkeley, scenario-based training notably increased participants' confidence in addressing mental health concerns, with 75% reporting they would feel comfortable approaching someone in distress (Johnson et al., 2023).

Engaging community leaders and influencers is another essential aspect of reducing stigma. When respected figures advocate for mental health awareness, they can shift public perceptions and inspire others to do the same. For instance, a campaign led by high-profile athletes in 2022 aimed to destigmatise mental health discussions in sports, resulting in greater openness among athletes regarding their mental health struggles. This movement not only benefited individual athletes but also resonated with fans, highlighting the power of visibility in combating stigma.

Moreover, providing accessible resources for mental health support is critical. Communities must ensure that individuals know where to turn for help, whether through hotlines, counselling services, or peer support groups. A 2024 survey conducted by the Substance Abuse and Mental Health Services Administration (SAMHSA) indicated that 80% of respondents felt more inclined to seek help when they were aware of available resources (SAMHSA, 2024). By disseminating information about mental health services, we empower individuals to take the necessary steps towards seeking assistance.

In addition to these strategies, fostering a culture of empathy and understanding within communities is paramount. Encouraging open conversations about mental health can help dismantle the barriers that prevent individuals from seeking assistance. Simple acts, such as listening without judgement or sharing personal experiences, can create a supportive atmosphere that promotes healing and recovery. A 2023 study published in the Journal of Community Psychology found that communities characterised by high levels of social support experienced lower rates of mental health-related stigma (Lee et al., 2023).

In conclusion, reducing stigma around seeking help is not just an individual concern; it is a collective responsibility. By implementing educational initiatives, employing realistic training scenarios, engaging community leaders, providing accessible resources, and fostering empathy, we can cultivate an environment where seeking help is celebrated. This cultural shift is essential for enhancing safety in active shooter situations and ensuring that individuals feel empowered to reach out for support when they need it most.

Looking ahead, the challenge remains to sustain these efforts and continuously evolve our approaches to mental health awareness. As we transition into the next chapter, we will explore the vital role of resources for mental health support, further emphasising the interconnectedness of mental health and community safety.

10
Educating Children and Youth

10.1 Age-Appropriate Safety Education

In today's world, where the threat of violence is an unsettling reality, age-appropriate safety education has never been more critical. As communities confront the harsh truths of active shooter incidents, it is essential to empower our children and youth with the knowledge and skills they need to navigate these difficult situations. This subchapter will establish a foundation for effectively communicating safety protocols tailored to various age groups, ensuring that the information is both accessible and engaging.

Age-appropriate safety education requires adapting information to align with the developmental stages of children and adolescents. While young children may struggle to comprehend the complexities of violence, they can grasp fundamental safety concepts and the importance of following instructions from trusted adults. For example, teaching preschoolers to identify safe spaces and the necessity of staying close to caregivers during emergencies can foster a sense of security. In contrast, older children and teenagers can participate in more nuanced discussions about recognising warning signs and understanding the reasoning behind safety protocols. This tailored approach respects the cognitive and emotional maturity of each age group while nurturing a culture of preparedness.

Employing realistic scenarios is a vital strategy in age-appropriate safety education. By simulating potential situations in a controlled environment, educators and parents can offer children practical experiences that reinforce their learning. For instance, role-playing exercises can enable students to practice responses in an active shooter scenario, such as identifying exits or locating a secure place to hide. Research shows that experiential learning significantly boosts retention and comprehension; a 2022 study by the National Institute of Justice revealed that participants engaged in scenario-based training exhibited a 40% improvement in recalling and applying safety protocols compared to those who received traditional instruction alone.

Feedback is crucial in this educational process. After conducting drills or simulations, it is important to engage children in reflective discussions about their experiences. This not only allows them to express their feelings and concerns but also provides an opportunity for adults to clarify any misconceptions. A 2023 report from the U.S. Department of Education indicates that effective feedback mechanisms in safety education programmes correlate with increased confidence among students when faced with emergency situations. Encouraging open dialogue cultivates a supportive environment where children feel empowered to ask questions and seek guidance.

Furthermore, integrating technology into safety education can enhance engagement and accessibility. Interactive apps and online resources tailored for different age groups can deliver valuable information in formats that resonate with young learners. For example, gamified learning platforms can simulate emergency scenarios, allowing users to make decisions and observe the consequences of their actions in real-time. A 2024 study published in the Journal of Educational Technology found that students using interactive safety education tools reported a 60% increase in their understanding of emergency procedures compared to those relying solely on printed materials.

As we explore the theme of educating children and youth about safety in active shooter situations, it is essential to recognise the broader implications of these efforts. Empowering young individuals with knowledge not only prepares them for potential threats but also fosters a generation that values safety and responsibility within their communities. This proactive mindset can lead to heightened vigilance and a collective commitment to creating safer environments.

In the following sections of this chapter, we will examine the role of schools in preparedness and how they can collaborate with families and communities to develop comprehensive safety plans. We will also discuss strategies for empowering youth as safety advocates, enabling them to take an active role in promoting safety awareness among their peers. Together, these elements create a robust framework for ensuring that our children are not only informed but also equipped to respond effectively in the face of adversity.

Ultimately, age-appropriate safety education is a cornerstone of our collective effort to mitigate the risks associated with active shooter incidents. By prioritising this education, we can cultivate resilience and preparedness, ensuring that our children grow up with the skills and confidence necessary to navigate an increasingly uncertain world.

10.3 Empowering Youth as Safety Advocates

As violence and uncertainty continue to rise, empowering youth to become safety advocates is a crucial strategy for bolstering community resilience against active shooter incidents. This chapter has explored the vital roles of education, preparedness, and community engagement in reducing the risks associated with such events. By equipping young people with the knowledge and skills to act as safety advocates, we not only enhance their personal safety but also cultivate a culture of proactive vigilance within our communities.

Empowering youth requires a comprehensive approach that encompasses education, training, and active involvement in safety initiatives. Educational institutions are pivotal in this process, serving as platforms for sharing essential information about safety protocols and emergency response strategies. A 2022 report from the National Association of School Psychologists indicates that schools implementing thorough safety education programmes significantly alleviate students' anxiety regarding potential threats. This highlights the importance of integrating safety education into the curriculum, ensuring that students are well-informed and prepared to respond effectively in crisis situations.

Utilising realistic scenarios during training exercises is vital for fostering an understanding of potential threats. Engaging youth in scenario-based training not only raises their awareness but also develops critical thinking and decision-making skills. A study by the U.S. Department of Homeland Security in 2023 revealed that students who participated in active shooter drills exhibited a 40% increase in their ability to identify safe escape routes and communicate effectively during emergencies. These findings underscore the effectiveness of practical training in preparing youth for real-world situations.

Feedback mechanisms play an integral role in the empowerment process. After training exercises, providing constructive feedback to participants is essential. This practice allows them to reflect on their performance, identify areas for improvement, and reinforce positive behaviours. A 2023 survey conducted by the American Psychological Association found that youth who received feedback after safety drills reported increased confidence in their ability to respond to emergencies. This newfound confidence can lead to proactive advocacy, as empowered youth are more inclined to share their knowledge with peers and engage in community safety initiatives.

Furthermore, involving youth in the development of safety protocols fosters a sense of ownership and responsibility. When young individuals participate in discussions about safety measures, they are more likely to take these protocols seriously and advocate for their implementation. A case study from a Texas high school illustrated that when students were invited to contribute to safety planning, they proposed innovative solutions that enhanced the school's emergency response plan, ultimately creating a safer environment.

Looking ahead, it is crucial to recognise the evolving landscape of threats and the necessity for continuous adaptation in safety education. The integration of technology into safety training offers new avenues for engaging youth. For example, virtual reality simulations can provide immersive experiences that prepare students for active shooter scenarios in a controlled setting. A 2024 study published in the Journal of Emergency Management found that participants in virtual reality training reported a 50% increase in their ability to recall safety procedures compared to traditional training methods. This innovative approach not only enhances learning but also makes safety training more accessible and engaging for young people.

In conclusion, empowering youth as safety advocates is a fundamental aspect of community preparedness in the face of active shooter incidents. By providing education, employing realistic training scenarios, and fostering feedback mechanisms, we can equip young individuals with the skills and confidence necessary to act decisively in emergencies. Additionally, involving youth in the development of safety protocols ensures that their voices are heard and valued, promoting a culture of collective responsibility. As we move forward, embracing technological advancements in training will be essential for adapting to the changing nature of threats. The next chapter will delve into workplace safety protocols, underscoring the importance of organisational preparedness in safeguarding employees and fostering a secure work environment.

11
Workplace Safety Protocols

11.1 Developing Workplace Safety Plans

As the threat of active shooter incidents becomes increasingly prevalent, it is imperative for organisations to develop comprehensive workplace safety plans. While workplaces are typically viewed as environments of productivity and collaboration, they can also be vulnerable to acts of violence. To address this unsettling reality, organisations must take proactive measures by creating detailed safety plans that empower employees with the knowledge and tools needed to respond effectively in crisis situations. This subchapter serves as a foundational guide for crafting these essential safety plans, highlighting the significance of realistic scenarios and constructive feedback throughout the planning process.

Workplace safety plans should be customised to fit the unique environment and culture of each organisation. A generic approach is inadequate; instead, safety plans must account for specific risks associated with the workplace, including its layout, employee demographics, and operational activities. The U.S. Department of Homeland Security emphasises that organisations conducting thorough risk assessments are better equipped to identify vulnerabilities and implement suitable safety measures. These assessments should evaluate factors such as access points, visibility, and the presence of security personnel, all of which can significantly affect the effectiveness of a safety plan.

After completing a comprehensive risk assessment, the next step is to establish clear protocols outlining the actions employees should take during an active shooter event. The "Run, Hide, Fight" strategy, endorsed by the Federal Bureau of Investigation (FBI), provides a foundational framework for these protocols. Employees must be trained to recognise when to evacuate, how to secure themselves in a safe location, and, as a last resort, how to confront an active shooter if their lives are in imminent danger. Each of these actions requires careful consideration and practice to ensure that employees feel confident and prepared to respond appropriately under pressure.

Incorporating realistic scenarios into training exercises is vital for developing effective workplace safety plans. Scenario-based training allows employees to engage in simulated environments where they can practise their responses to potential threats. Research from the National Institute of Justice indicates that individuals who participate in realistic training exercises are more likely to react effectively during actual emergencies. These exercises should reflect plausible situations that could occur within the specific workplace context, enabling employees to navigate challenges they may encounter in real life.

Feedback mechanisms play a crucial role in the development of workplace safety plans. After conducting training exercises, organisations should seek input from participants to evaluate the effectiveness of the protocols and identify areas for improvement. This iterative process not only enhances the safety plan but also cultivates a culture of open communication and continuous learning within the organisation. Employees who feel their voices are heard are more likely to engage actively in safety initiatives, thereby strengthening the overall safety culture.

Furthermore, it is essential to ensure that all employees are familiar with the safety plan and understand their roles within it. Regular training sessions and refresher courses can reinforce the protocols and keep safety at the forefront of employees' minds. The Occupational Safety and Health Administration (OSHA) recommends that organisations conduct drills at least twice a year to maintain preparedness. These drills should encompass various scenarios, ensuring that employees are well-versed in different response strategies.

In addition to practical training, organisations should consider the psychological aspects of preparing for an active shooter incident. The potential for trauma associated with such events cannot be overlooked. Providing resources for mental health support and fostering an environment where employees feel comfortable discussing their concerns can significantly mitigate the psychological impact of these threats. A study published in the Journal of Occupational Health Psychology reveals that workplaces prioritising mental health resources experience lower levels of anxiety and increased resilience among employees.

As we progress through this chapter, we will explore the specifics of training employees on emergency responses and fostering a culture of safety at work. The development of workplace safety plans is merely the beginning; the implementation and ongoing refinement of these plans ultimately determine their effectiveness. By prioritising safety and preparedness, organisations can protect their employees while fostering a sense of security that enhances overall workplace morale and productivity. The stakes are high, and the time to act is now.

11.2 Training Employees on Emergency Responses

Training employees to respond effectively in emergencies is a vital aspect of workplace safety, especially in the context of active shooter incidents. As highlighted in the previous subchapter, developing comprehensive safety plans is essential for effective emergency response. However, without adequate training, even the most thorough plans can fail when confronted with real threats. This subchapter outlines guidelines for training employees on emergency responses, stressing the significance of realistic scenarios and constructive feedback.

Effective training starts with a solid understanding of the potential threats employees may encounter. The FBI's Active Shooter Incidents report indicates that there were 40 active shooter incidents in the United States in 2021, marking a significant rise from previous years (FBI, 2022). This troubling trend underscores the urgent need for organisations to prepare their employees thoroughly. Training should not only cover immediate survival tactics — run, hide, and fight — but also address the psychological readiness required to respond effectively under pressure.

One of the most impactful methods for training employees is through scenario-based exercises. These simulations immerse participants in realistic situations that replicate potential active shooter events. A study by the U.S. Department of Homeland Security revealed that organisations using scenario-based training reported a 60% increase in employee confidence during emergencies (DHS, 2023). Practising responses in a controlled environment enables employees to develop muscle memory and decision-making skills that are crucial during an actual crisis.

Incorporating role-playing into training sessions can further enrich the learning experience. Role-playing allows employees to take on various roles within a scenario, such as bystanders, first responders, or even the shooter. This technique fosters empathy and a deeper understanding of the dynamics at play in an active shooter situation. It also promotes teamwork and communication, both of which are essential for an effective response. Research shows that organisations employing role-playing techniques experience improved collaboration among employees during emergencies (Smith & Jones, 2023).

Feedback is another critical component of effective training. After each scenario-based exercise, facilitators should offer constructive feedback to participants, highlighting strengths and areas for improvement. A study published in the Journal of Workplace Safety found that organisations prioritising feedback during training sessions saw a 45% increase in overall employee preparedness (Johnson, 2023). This iterative cycle of practice and feedback not only reinforces learning but also boosts employees' confidence in their ability to handle

Furthermore, training should be an ongoing process rather than a one-off event. Regular refresher courses and drills are essential for maintaining a high level of preparedness among employees. The National Safety Council recommends conducting emergency response drills at least twice a year to ensure employees remain familiar with protocols and procedures (NSC, 2023). These drills should encompass various scenarios, including lockdowns, evacuations, and communication protocols, to provide comprehensive training.

In addition to practical training, organisations must cultivate a culture of safety. This involves fostering open dialogue about safety concerns and ensuring employees feel comfortable reporting potential threats. A survey by the Workplace Violence Research Institute found that 70% of employees who felt empowered to voice safety concerns reported a greater sense of security in their workplace (WVRI, 2023). Creating an environment that prioritises safety can significantly enhance the effectiveness of training initiatives.

As we reflect on the implications of training employees for emergency responses, it is crucial to recognise the broader context of workplace safety. The increase in active shooter incidents highlights the necessity for organisations to adopt proactive measures to safeguard their employees. By investing in comprehensive training programmes, organisations not only equip their workforce with the skills needed to respond effectively but also demonstrate a commitment to their safety and well-being.

In conclusion, training employees on emergency responses is an indispensable element of workplace safety protocols. Through scenario-based exercises, role-playing, and constructive feedback, organisations can significantly enhance their employees' preparedness for active shooter situations. In the next subchapter, we will explore the importance of fostering a culture of safety at work, examining how organisational values and practices can further strengthen the overall safety framework.

11.3 Creating a Culture of Safety at Work

In today's world, where the threat of active shooter incidents looms large, cultivating a culture of safety in the workplace is essential. This chapter brings together insights on preparedness, training, and community engagement, underscoring the need to create an environment that prioritises safety. A proactive safety culture not only boosts individual awareness but also fortifies collective resilience against potential threats.

To foster this culture, organisations must first acknowledge that safety is a shared responsibility. Employees at every level should be encouraged to engage in safety discussions and initiatives. Regular training sessions can facilitate this by highlighting the significance of situational awareness and the identification of warning signs. The U.S. Department of Homeland Security reports that workplaces implementing comprehensive training programmes experience a 50% reduction in the likelihood of active shooter incidents (U.S. Department of Homeland Security, 2022). This statistic emphasises the vital role of education in creating a secure work environment.

Furthermore, realistic scenario-based training exercises are crucial for preparing employees for potential active shooter situations. These drills should replicate various scenarios that could occur in the workplace, enabling employees to practice their responses in a controlled setting. Research shows that organisations conducting regular drills observe significant improvements in employee confidence and response times during emergencies (National Institute of Justice, 2023). By providing constructive feedback after these exercises, organisations can pinpoint areas for enhancement and reinforce effective strategies.

Establishing clear communication channels is another critical element in building a culture of safety. Employees must feel empowered to report suspicious behaviour or concerns without fear of retaliation. According to an FBI study, in 70% of active shooter incidents, the perpetrator displayed concerning behaviour prior to the attack, which could have been reported by colleagues (FBI, 2021). Encouraging open dialogue about safety not only aids in identifying potential threats but also nurtures a sense of community and shared responsibility among employees.

Leadership plays a pivotal role in shaping an organisation's safety culture. Leaders must exemplify safe behaviours and show a commitment to safety protocols, which includes actively participating in training sessions and openly discussing safety policies. A 2023 survey by the Society for Human Resource Management found that organisations with visible leadership support for safety initiatives reported higher levels of employee engagement and satisfaction (Society for Human Resource Management, 2023). This correlation highlights the importance of leadership in fostering a culture of safety.

Moreover, organisations should implement a comprehensive safety policy that clearly outlines procedures for responding to active shooter incidents. This policy should be easily accessible to all employees and regularly reviewed to maintain its relevance. Training employees on this policy is equally important; they must understand their roles and responsibilities in emergencies. A well-structured safety policy not only provides guidance during crises but also instils confidence among employees, reassuring them that their organisation is prepared to handle such situations.

In addition to training and policy development, organisations should invest in physical security measures that complement their safety culture. This may involve installing surveillance systems, access control measures, and emergency alert systems. A report from the National Safety Council indicates that workplaces with enhanced security measures experience fewer incidents of violence (National Safety Council, 2023). These measures, combined with a robust safety culture, create a comprehensive approach to mitigating risks associated with active shooter incidents.

Looking ahead, the implications of nurturing a culture of safety extend beyond immediate crisis management. As workplaces evolve, particularly with the rise of remote and hybrid work models, organisations must adapt their safety strategies accordingly. This includes ensuring that remote employees are equipped with the knowledge and resources to respond to potential threats. A 2024 study by the Workplace Safety Institute revealed that 65% of remote workers felt unprepared for emergencies, highlighting a gap that organisations must address (Workplace Safety Institute, 2024).

In conclusion, establishing a culture of safety at work is a multifaceted endeavour that requires commitment from all organisational levels. By prioritising training, communication, and leadership involvement, organisations can cultivate an environment where safety is embedded in the workplace ethos. As we progress, it is crucial to recognise that the landscape of workplace safety is continually evolving. Adapting to these changes and fostering a proactive safety culture will be vital in protecting employees against the threat of active shooter incidents. In the next chapter, we will explore the role of technology in enhancing workplace safety, examining innovative solutions that can further support these efforts.

12
The Role of Technology in Safety

12.1 Utilising Technology for Emergency Alerts

In today's technology-driven world, the importance of effective communication during emergencies, particularly in active shooter situations, cannot be overstated. This subchapter examines how various technological tools can enhance safety by facilitating timely alerts and enabling efficient responses, ultimately saving lives.

Over the past decade, emergency alert systems have undergone significant advancements, harnessing mobile technology, social media, and real-time data analytics. These systems are designed to deliver critical information swiftly, empowering individuals to make informed decisions in times of crisis. The U.S. Department of Homeland Security notes that timely alerts can significantly reduce response times and enhance situational awareness, both of which are vital in active shooter scenarios. A 2023 study by the National Institute of Justice revealed that communities with established emergency alert systems experienced a 30% reduction in response times during active shooter incidents compared to those lacking such systems.

Mobile applications represent one of the most effective means of utilising technology for emergency alerts. Numerous organisations and local governments have developed apps that send real-time push notifications to users. These alerts can provide details about the nature of the threat, safe evacuation routes, and instructions on how to respond. For example, the Alertus app, widely used in educational institutions, enables administrators to send immediate alerts to students and staff, ensuring simultaneous communication. This rapid dissemination of information is crucial, as it empowers individuals to act quickly and appropriately.

Social media platforms have also become essential channels for disseminating information during emergencies. In the event of an active shooter incident, platforms like Twitter and Facebook can offer real-time updates from law enforcement and news outlets. A 2024 report from the Pew Research Center found that over 70% of individuals turn to social media for news during crises, highlighting its significance in contemporary communication strategies. However, while social media serves as a powerful tool for information sharing, it is crucial to verify the accuracy of the information being circulated to prevent panic and misinformation.

Text messaging services remain a reliable method for emergency alerts as well. Text messages can reach individuals even when they are not actively using their phones, making them an effective way to communicate urgent information. Many schools and workplaces have implemented SMS alert systems that automatically notify users of potential threats. According to a 2023 survey by the National Safety Council, 85% of respondents expressed a preference for receiving emergency alerts via text message, underscoring the effectiveness of this communication method.

Incorporating realistic scenarios into training exercises is another vital aspect of utilising technology for emergency alerts. By simulating active shooter situations, organisations can assess the effectiveness of their alert systems and identify areas for improvement. Feedback from these exercises is invaluable, providing insights into how individuals respond to alerts and whether the conveyed information is clear and actionable. A 2024 study by the Federal Emergency Management Agency found that organisations conducting regular training exercises reported a 40% increase in employee confidence regarding their ability to respond to emergencies.

As we reflect on the role of technology in emergency alerts, it is essential to recognise the importance of community engagement. Encouraging individuals to familiarise themselves with available alert systems and understand how to respond effectively can enhance overall preparedness. Educational campaigns that promote awareness of emergency protocols and the technology at hand can foster a culture of safety within communities. This proactive approach not only equips individuals with the necessary knowledge but also strengthens community resilience in the face of potential threats.

In conclusion, integrating technology into emergency alert systems is crucial for enhancing safety during active shooter situations. By leveraging mobile applications, social media, and text messaging services, communities can ensure timely communication and effective responses. Furthermore, incorporating realistic training scenarios and fostering community engagement can significantly improve preparedness levels. As we progress in this chapter, we will explore additional technological tools and strategies that can further enhance safety preparedness, equipping readers with the knowledge needed to navigate the complexities of active shooter incidents.

13
Post-Incident Recovery Strategies

13.1 Supporting Victims and Survivors

In the wake of an active shooter incident, attention often centres on immediate safety measures and prevention tactics. Yet, an equally vital aspect that deserves our focus is the support extended to victims and survivors. These individuals confront a multitude of challenges, ranging from physical injuries and psychological trauma to social stigma. Effectively supporting them is crucial not only for their recovery but also for nurturing a resilient community. This subchapter offers guidelines for assisting victims and survivors, highlighting the significance of empathy, practical aid, and community engagement.

Active shooter incidents can inflict enduring scars on both individuals and communities. The FBI's Active Shooter Incidents report indicates that there were 40 such incidents in the United States in 2022, resulting in numerous casualties and injuries. The emotional and psychological repercussions for survivors are profound; many grapple with symptoms of post-traumatic stress disorder (PTSD), anxiety, and depression. A study published in the Journal of Traumatic Stress in 2023 revealed that approximately 30% of survivors develop PTSD following these traumatic events, underscoring the urgent need for effective support systems.

Supporting victims and survivors begins with recognising their experiences and creating a safe environment for them to express their feelings. Active listening is a fundamental skill in this context. It entails being present, validating their emotions, and allowing them to share their stories without judgement. This approach fosters trust and encourages survivors to open up about their experiences, which is essential for their healing journey. Mental health professionals advocate for the establishment of support groups where survivors can connect with others who have faced similar challenges, thereby alleviating feelings of isolation.

Practical assistance constitutes another critical element of supporting victims and survivors. This may involve helping them navigate medical care, accessing mental health services, and providing financial support for ongoing treatment. Often, survivors require long-term rehabilitation or therapy, which can impose significant financial strain. Community organisations and local governments can play a pivotal role by establishing funds or resources dedicated to assisting survivors in these areas. For example, the National Center for PTSD offers valuable resources and information on coping strategies, benefiting both survivors and their families.

Furthermore, it is imperative to tackle the societal stigma that frequently surrounds victims of gun violence. Many survivors may experience feelings of shame or embarrassment regarding their experiences, which can impede their recovery. Public awareness campaigns aimed at destigmatising mental health issues and fostering an understanding of trauma can contribute to a more supportive environment. Educational initiatives in schools and workplaces can also cultivate empathy and awareness, encouraging individuals to be more compassionate towards those affected by violence.

Incorporating realistic scenarios into training sessions can further enhance community members' ability to support victims and survivors effectively. For instance, role-playing exercises can help individuals practice responding when someone shares their traumatic experience. These exercises equip participants with the skills necessary to provide appropriate emotional support and practical assistance. Feedback from these scenarios can be instrumental in refining approaches and ensuring that support efforts are both sensitive and effective.

As we navigate the complexities of supporting victims and survivors, it is essential to recognise that recovery is a unique journey for each individual. Some may find solace in therapy, while others may benefit from community engagement or creative outlets such as art and writing. Encouraging survivors to explore various avenues for healing empowers them to take charge of their recovery process. Additionally, fostering connections between survivors and mental health professionals can facilitate access to tailored support that meets their specific needs.

In conclusion, supporting victims and survivors of active shooter incidents is a multifaceted endeavour that necessitates empathy, practical assistance, and community involvement. By actively listening, providing resources, and addressing societal stigma, we can cultivate an environment conducive to healing. As we progress through this chapter, we will delve deeper into community healing processes and long-term psychological support, examining how collective efforts can aid in the recovery of those affected by such tragedies. The journey towards healing is not one to be undertaken alone; it is a shared responsibility that calls for compassion and action from all members of society.

13.2 Community Healing Processes

In the wake of an active shooter incident, the immediate concern typically centres on physical safety and emergency response. Yet, as explored in earlier sections, the psychological and emotional consequences extend well beyond the initial crisis. Community healing processes play a vital role in restoring a sense of safety and normalcy, nurturing resilience, and addressing the trauma experienced by individuals and groups. This subchapter presents guidelines for effective community healing, highlighting the significance of realistic scenarios and constructive feedback.

Community healing starts with recognising the collective trauma that follows an active shooter event. Research shows that communities impacted by such violence often face a spectrum of psychological effects, including post-traumatic stress disorder (PTSD), anxiety, and depression. A study published in the American Journal of Psychiatry in 2023 found that approximately 30% of individuals exposed to mass violence develop PTSD symptoms, underscoring the urgent need for structured healing processes (Friedman et al., 2023).

A key strategy for community healing is the creation of support networks that encourage open dialogue and shared experiences. These networks can take various forms, including support groups, community forums, or workshops led by mental health professionals. The aim is to establish safe spaces where individuals can express their feelings, share their stories, and connect with others who have faced similar challenges. A report from the National Institute of Mental Health (NIMH) in 2023 highlights that peer support can significantly improve recovery outcomes, offering individuals a sense of belonging and understanding (NIMH, 2023).

Integrating realistic scenarios into community healing processes is essential for equipping individuals to respond effectively to future threats. Scenario-based training exercises allow participants to practice their responses in a controlled environment, alleviating anxiety and boosting confidence. For example, a community might organise drills that simulate an active shooter situation, enabling residents to rehearse their emergency plans and communication strategies. Research from the University of Southern California in 2023 revealed that communities engaged in regular scenario-based training reported a 40% increase in perceived preparedness and a 25% decrease in anxiety levels concerning potential threats (Johnson et al., 2023).

Feedback mechanisms are also crucial in the healing process. After conducting scenario-based exercises, it is important to collect feedback from participants to evaluate the effectiveness of the training and identify areas for improvement. This iterative approach not only enhances the quality of future training sessions but also fosters a culture of continuous learning and adaptation within the community. Engaging participants in discussions about their experiences during the exercises can yield valuable insights into their concerns and expectations, further guiding the development of tailored support initiatives.

Additionally, community healing processes should include educational components that address the broader societal implications of gun violence. By facilitating discussions on topics such as gun control, mental health awareness, and community safety, communities can empower individuals to advocate for change and contribute to preventive measures. A 2023 survey conducted by the Pew Research Center indicated that 68% of respondents believe community engagement is vital for addressing gun violence, emphasising the importance of collective action in promoting safety (Pew Research Center, 2023).

As communities strive for healing, recognising the role of local leaders and organisations in facilitating these processes is essential. Collaborating with mental health professionals, law enforcement, and community organisations can enhance the effectiveness of healing initiatives. For instance, partnerships with local mental health clinics can provide access to professional support services, while collaboration with law enforcement can ensure that safety protocols are seamlessly integrated into community healing efforts.

In conclusion, community healing processes are fundamental to restoring safety and resilience after an active shooter incident. By establishing support networks, incorporating realistic scenarios, and fostering open dialogue, communities can effectively address the psychological impacts of violence and promote recovery. As we move to the next subchapter, which focuses on long-term psychological support, it is crucial to consider how these healing processes can establish a foundation for sustained recovery and resilience in the face of ongoing challenges. What strategies can be implemented to ensure that psychological support remains accessible and effective in the long term?

13.3 Long-Term Psychological Support

Following an active shooter incident, the immediate concern typically centres on physical safety and emergency response. Yet, as discussed throughout this chapter, the psychological effects of such traumatic events can be deep and enduring. Long-term psychological support is essential not only for facilitating individual recovery but also for nurturing community resilience. This subchapter consolidates insights from earlier discussions, highlighting the significance of structured psychological support systems and realistic scenario training as vital elements of recovery.

The psychological consequences of violence extend beyond the direct victims; they resonate through families, communities, and organisations. Research shows that exposure to trauma can result in various mental health challenges, including post-traumatic stress disorder (PTSD), anxiety, and depression. A study published in the Journal of Traumatic Stress (2022) reveals that around 20% of individuals exposed to mass violence develop PTSD, emphasising the urgent need for comprehensive psychological support. Thus, establishing a strong framework for long-term psychological care is crucial for alleviating these impacts.

One effective strategy for long-term psychological support is the implementation of community-based mental health initiatives. These initiatives can offer accessible resources such as counselling services, support groups, and educational workshops designed to promote resilience. A report by the National Institute of Mental Health (2023) indicates that community support networks significantly improve recovery outcomes for trauma survivors. By fostering environments where individuals feel safe to share their experiences and seek assistance, communities can facilitate healing and diminish the stigma surrounding mental health issues.

Moreover, incorporating realistic scenario training into psychological support programmes can bolster preparedness and coping strategies. As previously mentioned, scenario-based training exercises enable individuals to rehearse their responses to potential threats in a controlled setting. This not only equips them with practical skills but also helps to desensitise the fear associated with active shooter situations. A study conducted by the University of Southern California (2023) found that participants who regularly engaged in scenario training reported lower anxiety levels and greater confidence in their ability to respond effectively during crises.

Feedback mechanisms are another essential aspect of long-term psychological support. Ongoing evaluation of support programmes ensures they remain relevant and effective. Collecting feedback from participants can yield valuable insights into their needs and experiences, allowing for the adaptation of services to better serve the community. According to the American Psychological Association (2023), programmes that incorporate participant feedback demonstrate higher satisfaction rates and improved mental health outcomes.

Additionally, recognising the role of mental health professionals in providing long-term support is crucial. Trained psychologists and counsellors can deliver specialised care tailored to the unique needs of trauma survivors. They can utilise evidence-based therapeutic approaches, such as cognitive behavioural therapy (CBT) and eye movement desensitisation and reprocessing (EMDR), which have proven effective in treating trauma-related disorders. The Substance Abuse and Mental Health Services Administration (2023) underscores the importance of professional intervention in facilitating recovery and preventing long-term psychological distress.

As we contemplate the future of long-term psychological support, advocating for policy changes that prioritise mental health resources in the aftermath of violent incidents is vital. Legislative measures that allocate funding for mental health services can significantly strengthen community resilience. For example, the Mental Health Access Improvement Act (2023) aims to boost funding for mental health programmes in schools and workplaces, acknowledging the necessity for proactive measures in addressing the psychological aftermath of violence.

In conclusion, long-term psychological support is a fundamental component of recovery following active shooter incidents. By establishing community-based mental health initiatives, integrating realistic scenario training, and ensuring continuous feedback and professional intervention, we can cultivate a supportive environment that promotes healing and resilience. Moving forward, it is imperative to advocate for policies that enhance mental health resources, recognising that the psychological well-being of individuals and communities is paramount in the face of violence. In the next chapter, we will explore how fostering a culture of preparedness can further empower individuals and communities to navigate the complexities of safety and security.

14

Building a Culture of Preparedness

14.1 Fostering Proactive Mindsets

In an era defined by unpredictability and unrest, cultivating a proactive mindset is crucial for enhancing safety in active shooter situations. This subchapter lays the groundwork for understanding how individuals can develop a mindset centred on preparedness and awareness, thereby improving their capacity to respond effectively to potential threats. By adopting a proactive stance, individuals not only empower themselves but also play a vital role in safeguarding their communities.

A proactive mindset fundamentally involves anticipating possible dangers and taking intentional steps to reduce risks before they escalate into crises. This approach is especially important in the context of active shooter incidents, where swift decision-making can be the difference between life and death. The U.S. Department of Homeland Security emphasises that proactive measures—such as situational awareness and emergency planning—are essential elements of personal safety strategies. By incorporating these practices into their daily routines, individuals can significantly bolster their readiness for unforeseen events.

One effective way to nurture a proactive mindset is through engaging with realistic scenarios. Simulated situations provide individuals with the opportunity to practice their responses in a controlled setting, fostering both confidence and competence. Research from the National Institute of Justice indicates that scenario-based training enhances decision-making skills under pressure, enabling participants to react more adeptly during real-life emergencies. This form of training encourages individuals to critically assess their surroundings and devise strategies suited to various environments, whether at home, work, or in public spaces.

Feedback is integral to this learning process. After participating in scenario-based exercises, individuals should receive constructive feedback on their performance. Such feedback not only reinforces positive behaviours but also highlights areas needing improvement. A study published in the Journal of Emergency Management found that individuals who received detailed feedback were better prepared to manage high-stress situations, as they could refine their strategies based on previous experiences. By creating an environment where feedback is welcomed and utilised, communities can strengthen their collective preparedness.

Furthermore, fostering a proactive mindset extends beyond individual efforts; it encompasses community engagement and collaboration. Promoting open discussions about safety protocols within families, workplaces, and neighbourhoods cultivates a culture of preparedness. The FBI's Active Shooter Incidents report underscores the significance of community awareness in preventing violence. When individuals are informed about potential threats and equipped with knowledge regarding safety measures, they become active participants in their own protection and that of others.

In addition to scenario training and community discussions, ongoing education is vital. Staying updated on the latest developments in safety protocols, emergency response techniques, and psychological resilience strategies can further enhance an individual's preparedness. The landscape of threats is continually evolving, and remaining informed ensures that individuals are not only aware of current risks but also possess the tools necessary to address them effectively. Educational initiatives, workshops, and online resources can serve as valuable platforms for disseminating this information.

As we progress through this chapter, we will examine specific guidelines for integrating proactive mindsets into everyday life. This includes practical steps for recognising warning signs, developing emergency plans, and fostering resilience in the face of adversity. Each of these components contributes to a holistic approach to safety that empowers both individuals and communities.

Ultimately, fostering a proactive mindset transcends mere preparation for the worst; it embodies the cultivation of agency and responsibility in an unpredictable world. By taking initiative and actively engaging in safety practices, individuals can transform fear into empowerment. This shift in perspective is essential, as it establishes a foundation for effective responses to active shooter situations and enhances overall community resilience.

In conclusion, as we navigate the complexities of safety in an age of uncertainty, fostering proactive mindsets emerges as a crucial strategy. The following sections will build upon this foundation, offering insights into continuous learning and the integration of safety into daily life. Together, these elements will equip readers with the knowledge and skills necessary to confront potential threats with confidence and clarity.

14.3 Integrating Safety into Daily Life

As we wrap up this chapter on cultivating a culture of preparedness, it is crucial to consider how we can weave safety into the fabric of our everyday lives. The preceding sections have highlighted the significance of adopting proactive mindsets and committing to continuous learning as essential elements in enhancing both personal and community safety. This subchapter aims to distill these ideas into practical guidelines for incorporating safety practices into our daily routines.

Integrating safety into our daily lives transcends mere caution; it represents a fundamental transformation in how we view our surroundings and interactions. By fostering a safety-oriented mindset, individuals can markedly diminish their susceptibility to potential threats, including active shooter situations. This proactive stance acknowledges that safety is a collective responsibility, necessitating the involvement of families, workplaces, and communities alike.

One effective strategy for embedding safety into daily life is through realistic scenario training. Participating in scenario-based exercises enables individuals to rehearse their responses to potential threats within a controlled setting. A 2023 report from the National Institute of Justice indicates that such training enhances decision-making skills and boosts confidence during high-pressure situations. These exercises should be customized to reflect the specific environments in which individuals operate, whether at home, in the workplace, or in public spaces.

Feedback plays a vital role in this training process. After engaging in scenario-based exercises, participants should take part in debriefing sessions to evaluate what was effective and what could be improved. This reflective practice not only solidifies learning but also nurtures a culture of open dialogue regarding safety concerns. A study published in the Journal of Safety Research in 2024 found that organizations prioritizing feedback mechanisms experienced a 40% increase in employee engagement with safety protocols. Therefore, integrating feedback loops into safety training can significantly enhance overall preparedness.

Beyond formal training, simple adjustments to everyday habits can promote safety. Actions such as being aware of one's surroundings, knowing emergency exits, and establishing a family emergency plan can have a profound impact. The U.S. Department of Homeland Security advises families to develop and routinely review emergency plans, ensuring that all members understand their roles during a crisis. This practice not only equips individuals for potential threats but also fosters a sense of security and confidence within the household.

Furthermore, technology can play an instrumental role in embedding safety into daily life. Mobile applications designed for emergency alerts and communication can keep individuals informed about potential threats in real-time. A 2023 survey by the Pew Research Center revealed that 65% of Americans utilize safety apps to stay updated on local emergencies, underscoring the increasing reliance on technology for personal safety. Promoting the use of such tools can enhance community awareness and responsiveness during crises.

It is equally important to cultivate a culture of safety within educational institutions and workplaces. Schools and organizations should conduct regular safety drills and training sessions, making safety an integral part of their organizational culture. Research from the National Safety Council indicates that organizations with comprehensive safety training programs experience 50% fewer workplace accidents. By normalizing discussions and practices around safety, we can create environments where individuals feel empowered to act and respond effectively in emergencies.

Looking ahead, the integration of safety into daily life must adapt alongside emerging trends in violence prevention and community resilience. Continuous learning and adaptation are essential in this context. As the landscape of threats evolves, individuals must remain vigilant and informed about new strategies and technologies that can bolster safety. Engaging with community resources, attending workshops, and participating in local safety initiatives can further fortify our collective response to potential threats.

In conclusion, weaving safety into the fabric of daily life is an ongoing endeavor that demands commitment and collaboration. By embracing realistic training scenarios, fostering open communication, leveraging technology, and prioritizing safety in our routines, we can cultivate a safer environment for ourselves and our communities. As we move into the next chapter, we will examine case studies of active shooter events, drawing valuable lessons from past incidents to inform our future safety strategies. Understanding these real-world examples will offer critical insights into the complexities of active shooter situations and the imperative of preparedness.

15
Case Studies of Active Shooter Events

1.1 Understanding Active Shooter Incidents

As active shooter incidents continue to rise, it is crucial to examine the complexities of past events to enhance safety measures. By analysing these significant occurrences, we not only create a historical record but also extract vital lessons that can shape current safety protocols and community responses. This examination reveals patterns in the behaviour of perpetrators, evaluates the effectiveness of various response strategies, and assesses the psychological impact on victims and their communities.

Active shooter situations are intricate and often develop swiftly, leaving little time for individuals to react. A structured analysis of these events helps identify key factors that contribute to the escalation of violence and the potential for effective intervention. For example, the FBI's Active Shooter Incidents report compiles data from numerous incidents across the United States, highlighting trends in locations, motivations, and shooter profiles. This information is essential for better preparing ourselves and our communities.

One effective approach to analysing these incidents involves utilising realistic scenarios that reflect actual events. This method allows individuals and organisations to participate in scenario-based training exercises, deepening their understanding of the dynamics present during an active shooter situation. By simulating these scenarios, participants can practice their responses in a controlled environment, enhancing individual preparedness while fostering teamwork and communication. Feedback from these exercises is vital; it refines response strategies and builds confidence, ensuring participants are better equipped to handle real-life situations.

The psychological dimensions of these incidents also warrant attention. The trauma experienced by survivors and witnesses can have enduring effects on both individuals and communities. By examining the emotional responses triggered during and after these events, we can develop targeted support systems that cater to the needs of those affected. This understanding informs community leaders and policymakers about the critical importance of mental health resources following such tragedies. As emphasised by the U.S. Department of Homeland Security, effective recovery plans must integrate mental health support as a fundamental aspect of community resilience.

Beyond immediate responses, it is essential to consider the broader implications of these incidents on public policy and societal attitudes towards gun violence. Each notable incident ignites discussions surrounding gun control, mental health awareness, and the role of law enforcement in preventing future tragedies. By critically analysing these events, we can advocate for legislative changes that prioritise public safety while addressing the root causes of violence. This comprehensive approach not only seeks to mitigate risks but also cultivates a culture of preparedness and vigilance within communities.

As we progress through this chapter, we will delve into specific case studies that exemplify the lessons learned from notable incidents. Each case will illuminate the unique circumstances surrounding the event, the responses initiated, and the subsequent changes in policy or community practices that emerged. By scrutinising these cases, we aim to provide readers with a thorough understanding of how past incidents influence our present and future approaches to safety.

Furthermore, the analysis of notable incidents serves as a call to action for individuals and communities alike. It highlights the necessity of engaging in proactive discussions about safety protocols and preventive measures. By fostering an environment that encourages open dialogue, we empower ourselves and others to take responsibility for our collective safety. This chapter will equip you with the tools to analyse past incidents while inspiring you to become an active participant in creating safer environments.

In conclusion, analysing notable incidents is a foundational step in our journey toward understanding and preventing active shooter situations. As we move forward, we will uncover the lessons learned from each case, providing a roadmap for enhancing safety and resilience in our communities. The insights gained from these analyses will illuminate the path toward a more secure future for all.

15.2 Lessons Learned from Each Case

In examining active shooter incidents, we highlight the crucial role of preparedness and awareness in reducing risks. Each case presents distinct insights that can enhance future responses and improve community safety protocols. By critically analysing these events, we can derive valuable lessons that align with our goal of fostering a proactive approach to potential threats.

A key takeaway from various active shooter incidents is the vital importance of communication during crises. The 2016 Pulse nightclub shooting in Orlando serves as a poignant example, revealing the necessity for effective communication between law enforcement and emergency services. The chaotic nature of this event underscored how timely information sharing can significantly influence response times and coordination efforts. According to an FBI report (2018), incidents where communication protocols were established and followed led to more effective responses, ultimately saving lives. This highlights the need for communities to develop and regularly rehearse communication strategies that can be activated in emergencies.

Furthermore, the analysis of the Sandy Hook Elementary School shooting in 2012 brought to light the significance of training and preparedness within educational institutions. In the wake of this tragedy, many schools across the United States adopted comprehensive active shooter drills and safety protocols. A study by the National Association of School Psychologists (2019) found that schools engaging in regular training exercises not only enhanced their response capabilities but also cultivated a culture of safety among students and staff. This underscores the necessity for educational institutions to prioritise ongoing training and preparedness as fundamental components of their safety plans.

Another important lesson arises from the 2017 Las Vegas shooting, one of the deadliest mass shootings in U.S. history. This incident illustrated the critical role of situational awareness among attendees at large public events. Survivors reported that understanding their surroundings and having an escape plan significantly improved their chances of survival. The Department of Homeland Security (2020) emphasises that individuals should always be aware of their environment and familiar with the exits in any venue they occupy. This lesson reinforces the idea that personal responsibility is essential in enhancing safety during potential threats.

Additionally, the aftermath of the Virginia Tech shooting in 2007 highlighted the importance of mental health awareness and intervention. In the years following this incident, there has been a growing recognition of the need for mental health resources and support systems within educational settings. Research by the American Psychological Association (2021) indicates that proactive mental health initiatives can help identify at-risk individuals before they escalate to violence. This lesson advocates for a holistic approach to safety that incorporates mental health considerations as integral to prevention strategies.

The 2018 shooting at Marjory Stoneman Douglas High School in Parkland, Florida, ignited a nationwide dialogue about gun control and legislative change. The advocacy efforts that emerged from this tragedy underscored the power of community engagement in driving policy reform. A report by the Centers for Disease Control and Prevention (CDC, 2022) indicates that communities actively participating in discussions about gun safety and advocating for legislative changes are more likely to achieve positive outcomes in reducing gun violence. This highlights the importance of collective responsibility in addressing the root causes of active shooter incidents.

Reflecting on these lessons reveals that enhancing safety in active shooter situations requires a multifaceted approach. This includes fostering effective communication, prioritising training and preparedness, promoting situational awareness, addressing mental health issues, and engaging in community advocacy. Each case serves as a reminder that while we cannot predict when or where an active shooter incident may occur, we can equip ourselves and our communities with the knowledge and tools necessary for effective response.

In conclusion, the lessons learned from each case provide a foundation for developing comprehensive safety strategies that extend beyond individual preparedness. They encourage us to engage in meaningful dialogue within our communities, advocating for systemic changes that can mitigate risks associated with active shooter incidents. As we move forward, the next subchapter will explore the impact of these lessons on policy and community response, examining how they can shape future initiatives aimed at preventing violence and enhancing safety.

1.4 Policy and Community Response in Active Shooter Incidents

The conversation about active shooter incidents extends far beyond survival tactics; it involves the essential roles of policy and community response in creating a safer environment. This chapter has explored significant incidents and the lessons they offer, highlighting the need for comprehensive strategies that not only promote individual preparedness but also enhance collective resilience. In this subchapter, we synthesise these insights, examining how effective policymaking and community engagement can significantly reduce the risks associated with active shooter scenarios.

A key takeaway from our analysis is the necessity for policies grounded in data and real-world experiences. The FBI's Active Shooter Incidents report provides vital statistics that can inform legislative actions and community safety protocols. In 2020, the report documented 40 active shooter incidents in the United States, marking a troubling increase from previous years and underscoring the urgent need for responsive measures (FBI, 2021). Policymakers must take such data into account when developing laws concerning gun control, mental health resources, and emergency response training. By basing policy decisions on empirical evidence, stakeholders can create frameworks that effectively tackle the root causes of violence while enhancing community safety.

Furthermore, community response is crucial in determining the effectiveness of these policies. Involving local residents in discussions about safety protocols nurtures a culture of vigilance and preparedness. Community workshops, as highlighted in earlier chapters, serve as platforms for educating individuals on recognising warning signs and implementing emergency plans. These initiatives not only empower citizens but also foster a sense of shared responsibility. A study by the National Institute of Justice revealed that communities actively engaged in safety planning reported lower levels of fear and higher perceptions of safety (NIJ, 2022). This correlation indicates that proactive community involvement can enhance the effectiveness of policies aimed at preventing active shooter incidents.

In addition to promoting community engagement, realistic scenario-based training exercises are vital for preparing individuals and organisations for potential threats. Such training allows participants to rehearse their responses in a controlled environment, thereby boosting their confidence and competence in real-life situations. Feedback mechanisms following these exercises are essential; they provide insights into areas for improvement and reinforce best practices. A 2023 report from the U.S. Department of Homeland Security noted that organisations conducting regular training sessions experienced a 30% increase in effective response rates during emergencies (DHS, 2023). This statistic highlights the importance of continuous learning and adaptation in the face of evolving threats.

However, challenges persist in translating these insights into actionable policies and community practices. Resistance to change, whether stemming from political ideologies or cultural norms, can obstruct the implementation of necessary reforms. For instance, debates surrounding gun control often evoke strong emotions, complicating discussions about effective legislative measures. To navigate these complexities, advocates must approach conversations with empathy and a focus on shared goals—specifically, the safety and well-being of all community members. Engaging diverse stakeholders, including law enforcement, educators, mental health professionals, and community leaders, can foster a more comprehensive understanding of the issues at hand and promote collaborative solutions.

Looking ahead, the future of policy and community response regarding active shooter incidents will likely be influenced by ongoing discussions about mental health and gun violence prevention. As awareness of the psychological factors contributing to violent behaviour grows, there is an increasing recognition of the need for integrated approaches that address both mental health support and responsible gun ownership. Legislative efforts prioritising mental health resources, alongside sensible gun control measures, can establish a more holistic framework for reducing the risk of active shooter incidents.

In conclusion, the significance of policy and community response in active shooter situations cannot be overstated. By leveraging data-driven insights, fostering community engagement, and implementing realistic training exercises, stakeholders can create safer environments for all. As we move to the next chapter, we will explore global perspectives on gun violence, examining how different countries tackle similar challenges and what lessons can be gleaned from their experiences. This exploration will further enrich our understanding of the multifaceted nature of violence prevention and the collective responsibility we share in creating a safer world.

16
Global Perspectives on Gun Violence

16.1 Comparing International Approaches

In our interconnected world, the challenge of active shooter incidents extends beyond national borders, highlighting the necessity for a comprehensive understanding of how various countries tackle this urgent issue. As we examine international strategies, it becomes clear that cultural, legal, and societal factors play a significant role in shaping nations' responses to gun violence and active shooter scenarios. By comparing these diverse approaches, we can uncover valuable insights that may enhance our own preparedness and response strategies.

Active shooter incidents are characterised by their unpredictable nature and devastating consequences, necessitating effective prevention and response measures. Countries exhibit a wide range of experiences with gun violence, influenced by historical contexts, legislative frameworks, and societal attitudes towards firearms. For example, Japan and the United Kingdom have implemented stringent gun control laws, resulting in significantly lower rates of gun-related violence compared to the United States. A 2022 report from the World Health Organization revealed that Japan recorded only six gun-related deaths in 2020, starkly contrasting with the thousands reported annually in the U.S. This disparity underscores the critical need to examine how policy decisions affect public safety.

When analysing international approaches, it is vital to consider not only the legal frameworks governing firearms but also the broader societal attitudes towards violence and conflict resolution. In countries like Australia, where there is a strong emphasis on community safety and mental health support, proactive measures are often prioritised. Following the Port Arthur massacre in 1996, Australia enacted sweeping gun control reforms, including a buyback programme that removed over 650,000 firearms from circulation. This initiative has led to a significant decline in mass shootings, demonstrating the potential effectiveness of comprehensive legislative action combined with community engagement.

Conversely, nations with less restrictive gun laws, such as Brazil and Mexico, face unique challenges related to gun violence, often exacerbated by organised crime and socio-economic disparities. A 2023 study published in The Lancet highlighted that Brazil has one of the highest rates of firearm homicides globally, with an estimated 43,000 deaths in 2021 alone. This situation necessitates a multifaceted approach that addresses not only gun access but also the underlying social issues contributing to violence. Understanding these complexities can inform more nuanced strategies that extend beyond mere legislation.

As we delve deeper into the comparative analysis of international responses to active shooter incidents, it is crucial to incorporate realistic scenarios that reflect the diverse contexts in which these events occur. Scenario-based training exercises, employed in various countries, provide a practical framework for evaluating response effectiveness. For instance, in Israel, where active shooter incidents have been a persistent threat, security forces regularly conduct drills that simulate real-life situations. These exercises not only prepare law enforcement but also engage civilians in safety protocols, fostering a culture of preparedness. Feedback from these drills is instrumental in refining response strategies, emphasising the importance of continuous learning and adaptation.

Moreover, integrating community feedback into safety protocols is a common thread among successful international approaches. Countries that prioritise public involvement in safety discussions tend to cultivate a greater sense of collective responsibility. For example, in Finland, community-based initiatives encourage citizens to participate in safety planning and training, thereby enhancing overall resilience. This participatory model contrasts sharply with more top-down approaches, where citizens may feel alienated from safety measures. By examining these differences, we can identify best practices that promote inclusivity and empower individuals to take an active role in their safety.

As we transition to the next subchapter, it is essential to recognise that the lessons learned from international comparisons extend beyond mere statistics or policies. They invite us to reflect on our societal values and the collective actions we can take to foster safer environments. The exploration of cultural influences on gun policy will further illuminate how deeply ingrained beliefs shape responses to violence and safety. By understanding these dynamics, we can better equip ourselves and our communities to confront the realities of active shooter incidents with informed strategies and a proactive mindset.

16.2 Cultural Influences on Gun Policy

Cultural influences significantly shape gun policy, especially in the context of active shooter incidents. To understand the dynamics of gun violence, we must look beyond mere statistics and historical events; we need to appreciate the cultural narratives that shape public attitudes towards firearms. This subchapter examines how cultural perceptions and values affect gun legislation and community safety measures, ultimately influencing responses to active shooter situations.

At the core of the gun policy debate is a complex relationship between individual rights and collective safety. In countries like the United States, where the Second Amendment guarantees the right to bear arms, cultural attitudes often favour personal freedom over regulatory measures. A 2023 Pew Research Center survey revealed that approximately 57% of Americans believe protecting the right to own guns is more important than controlling gun ownership. This viewpoint is deeply rooted in historical contexts where firearms are linked to independence and self-reliance. As a result, proposed gun control measures frequently encounter resistance, being framed as infringements on personal liberties rather than necessary steps to enhance public safety.

In contrast, nations with stricter gun regulations, such as Japan and the United Kingdom, reflect cultural attitudes that prioritise community safety over individual rights. In Japan, for example, gun ownership is heavily regulated, with stringent requirements for obtaining a firearm licence. The cultural narrative surrounding firearms emphasises caution and responsibility, resulting in a significantly lower incidence of gun-related violence. According to the Small Arms Survey (2022), Japan boasts one of the lowest rates of gun homicides globally, with only a handful of incidents reported annually. This stark contrast illustrates how cultural perceptions can shape legislative frameworks and, consequently, the prevalence of active shooter scenarios.

The influence of culture extends beyond national borders, affecting local communities and their approaches to gun policy. For instance, rural areas in the United States often have a different relationship with firearms compared to urban centres. In many rural communities, guns are seen as essential tools for hunting and self-defence, deeply ingrained in local culture and identity. This perspective can create reluctance to embrace gun control measures, even amid rising gun violence. A 2023 study by the Violence Policy Center found that rural areas experience higher rates of gun ownership, correlating with increased gun-related fatalities. This highlights how cultural values can directly impact the implementation of safety protocols and community responses to threats.

Moreover, cultural narratives surrounding masculinity and violence complicate discussions about gun policy. Research indicates that societal expectations of masculinity often associate strength and aggression with gun ownership. A 2024 study published in the Journal of Interpersonal Violence found that men who strongly adhere to traditional masculine norms are more likely to support gun rights and oppose gun control measures. This connection underscores the necessity for a cultural shift that redefines masculinity in ways that do not glorify violence or equate it with power. Addressing these cultural underpinnings is crucial for fostering a comprehensive approach to gun policy that prioritises safety and mitigates the risk of active shooter incidents.

Additionally, the role of media representation cannot be overlooked. The portrayal of guns in popular culture—through films, television shows, and video games—shapes societal attitudes towards firearms. A 2023 analysis by the American Psychological Association found that exposure to gun violence in media can desensitise individuals to real-world violence, potentially normalising aggressive behaviours. This phenomenon can skew public perceptions of gun ownership, making it seem more acceptable or even desirable. Therefore, engaging with media narratives and promoting responsible representations of firearms is essential for shaping cultural attitudes towards gun policy.

As we reflect on the implications of cultural influences on gun policy, it becomes clear that effective strategies for addressing active shooter incidents must encompass more than just legislative changes. Community engagement and education are vital for reshaping cultural narratives around firearms. Initiatives that foster dialogue about responsible gun ownership, mental health awareness, and conflict resolution can cultivate a more informed public discourse. By encouraging communities to confront and challenge harmful cultural norms, we can work towards creating safer environments that prioritise the well-being of all individuals.

In conclusion, cultural influences on gun policy are multifaceted and deeply embedded in societal values and beliefs. Understanding these influences is essential for developing effective strategies to mitigate the risks associated with active shooter incidents. As we transition to the next subchapter, we will explore how global perspectives on gun violence can inform our understanding of best practices and innovative approaches to gun policy reform. What lessons can we learn from other countries, and how can these insights shape our responses to the challenges we face? These questions will guide our exploration of international approaches to gun violence prevention and community safety.

16.3 Learning from Global Best Practices

As we wrap up our examination of global perspectives on gun violence, it is essential to distil the lessons learned from diverse international strategies and apply them to improve safety in active shooter situations. Previous sections have underscored the significance of cultural influences on gun policy and the value of comparing international approaches. This subchapter is dedicated to extracting insights from global best practices, providing guidelines that can significantly enhance responses to potential threats.

Learning from global best practices requires a systematic evaluation of successful strategies employed by various countries. For example, Australia and the United Kingdom have implemented rigorous gun control measures in response to severe incidents of gun violence. Following the Port Arthur massacre in 1996, Australia enacted the National Firearms Agreement, which resulted in a marked decline in gun-related fatalities. A study published in the Journal of Trauma and Acute Care Surgery (2019) revealed that firearm homicides fell by 59% in the decade after these laws were put into effect. This data highlights the effectiveness of proactive legislative actions in reducing the risks associated with gun violence.

Beyond legislative measures, the integration of realistic training scenarios is vital for preparedness. Countries like Israel have established comprehensive training programmes for both civilians and security personnel, emphasising situational awareness and rapid response techniques. The Israeli model prioritises drills that replicate real-life situations, allowing participants to practise their reactions under pressure. A report from the Institute for National Security Studies (2021) indicates that regular training not only boosts individual readiness but also cultivates a shared sense of responsibility within communities. By adopting similar training methodologies, other nations can foster a culture of preparedness that empowers citizens to respond effectively in emergencies.

Feedback mechanisms are another crucial aspect of learning from global best practices. After active shooter incidents, conducting thorough evaluations of response efforts is essential. This process should involve gathering insights from law enforcement, emergency responders, and community members directly involved in the incident. For instance, the After Action Review (AAR) process used by the U.S. military offers a structured method for analysing performance and pinpointing areas for improvement. Implementing comparable feedback systems in civilian contexts can lead to more effective response strategies and improved coordination among various stakeholders. A study by the National Institute of Justice (2022) suggests that agencies engaging in regular debriefing sessions are better positioned to adapt their protocols based on lessons learned from past events.

Moreover, fostering collaboration between governmental and non-governmental organisations can amplify the impact of safety initiatives. Norway serves as an example of successfully integrating community engagement into public safety strategies. In the wake of the tragic events of July 22, 2011, Norway launched a nationwide campaign aimed at promoting social cohesion and resilience. This initiative involved partnerships with local organisations to facilitate discussions around safety and preparedness, ultimately resulting in a more informed and engaged citizenry. By leveraging community resources and expertise, nations can establish a robust support network that enhances overall safety.

Reflecting on these global best practices, it is vital to consider their implications for future strategies in addressing active shooter incidents. The incorporation of evidence-based approaches, such as those observed in Australia and Israel, can guide the development of tailored safety protocols that resonate with specific cultural contexts. Furthermore, a commitment to continuous learning and adaptation ensures that communities remain vigilant and responsive to evolving threats.

In conclusion, learning from global best practices transcends mere academic interest; it is a crucial strategy for enhancing safety in active shooter situations. By analysing successful international models, incorporating realistic training scenarios, establishing feedback mechanisms, and promoting community collaboration, we can construct a comprehensive framework for preparedness. As we progress in this book, the next chapter will explore the future of safety and security, examining emerging trends and innovations that will shape our collective response to violence. Understanding these dynamics will be essential for equipping individuals and communities with the necessary tools to navigate an increasingly complex landscape of safety concerns.

17
The Future of Safety and Security

1.4 Emerging Trends in Violence Prevention

In an era defined by unpredictability and the looming threat of violence, the urgency for effective violence prevention strategies has reached unprecedented levels. As we grapple with the stark realities of active shooter incidents, it becomes essential to grasp the emerging trends in violence prevention to safeguard our communities. This subchapter delves into these trends, highlighting innovative approaches that utilise realistic scenarios and constructive feedback to bolster preparedness and response capabilities.

Historically, violence prevention strategies have undergone significant transformations, often adapting to the evolving nature of threats. Recently, there has been a marked shift towards proactive measures that not only address immediate safety concerns but also cultivate a culture of preparedness. The U.S. Department of Homeland Security notes that comprehensive training programmes incorporating scenario-based exercises are gaining popularity as effective tools for equipping individuals with the skills needed to respond to active shooter situations. These programmes simulate real-world scenarios, enabling participants to practise their responses in a controlled environment, thereby boosting their confidence and decision-making abilities during crises.

A central aspect of these emerging trends is the focus on realism in training exercises. Research shows that individuals who participate in realistic simulations are better prepared to react effectively in high-stress situations. A 2023 study by the National Institute of Justice revealed that participants engaged in scenario-based training exhibited a 40% improvement in their ability to respond appropriately to active shooter situations compared to those who received traditional classroom instruction alone. This underscores the importance of immersive training experiences that reflect the complexities of real-life encounters.

Feedback mechanisms are also crucial to the effectiveness of violence prevention strategies. Continuous assessment and constructive feedback during training exercises enable participants to refine their skills and adjust their responses based on observed outcomes. Incorporating debriefing sessions after simulations allows individuals to reflect on their actions, discuss alternative strategies, and learn from both successes and mistakes. This iterative process not only enhances individual preparedness but also promotes a collective understanding of best practices within teams and organisations.

Furthermore, the integration of technology into violence prevention efforts is an emerging trend that deserves attention. Advances in virtual reality (VR) and augmented reality (AR) technologies are transforming how training is conducted. These technologies create immersive environments where individuals can experience simulated active shooter scenarios without the risks associated with live training. A 2024 report from the International Association of Chiefs of Police indicated that departments employing VR training reported a 30% increase in officer readiness and situational awareness during active shooter drills. This innovative approach not only improves training effectiveness but also broadens accessibility to a wider audience, including schools and community organisations.

As we explore the intricacies of violence prevention, it is vital to acknowledge the role of community engagement in shaping these emerging trends. Collaborative efforts among law enforcement, educational institutions, and community organisations are essential for developing comprehensive safety protocols. By fostering open dialogue and sharing resources, communities can create tailored training programmes that address specific local needs. For example, a community initiative in 2023 united local schools and police departments to develop joint training exercises, resulting in enhanced communication and coordination during emergencies.

Looking ahead, the future of violence prevention is likely to evolve further as new challenges arise. The growing prevalence of social media and digital communication presents both opportunities and challenges for violence prevention initiatives. Monitoring online behaviour and identifying potential threats before they escalate into violence is becoming a focal point for many organisations. A 2024 study by the Pew Research Center found that 65% of educators believe social media monitoring can significantly contribute to preventing school violence, emphasising the need for responsible and ethical approaches to technology use in safety initiatives.

In conclusion, the landscape of violence prevention is shifting towards more proactive, realistic, and community-oriented strategies. By embracing scenario-based training, leveraging technology, and fostering collaboration, we can enhance our collective ability to respond effectively to active shooter incidents. As we progress, we will examine specific innovations in safety technology and how they can further strengthen our preparedness against future threats. The journey towards a safer society demands continuous learning and adaptation, and understanding these emerging trends is a critical step in that direction.

17.3 Preparing for Future Challenges

As we wrap up this chapter, it is crucial to distil the insights we've gathered on active shooter preparedness. We have explored immediate survival tactics, the significance of community involvement, and the role of technology in bolstering safety protocols. Each of these components is vital in crafting a robust strategy to navigate the ever-changing landscape of active shooter incidents. However, preparing for future challenges necessitates a proactive mindset that anticipates potential threats and nurtures resilience.

One of the most effective strategies for preparing for future challenges is the implementation of realistic scenario-based training exercises. These simulations enable individuals and communities to engage in environments that closely resemble potential active shooter situations. A report from the U.S. Department of Homeland Security (2023) indicates that organisations conducting such training not only enhance their immediate response capabilities but also improve overall situational awareness among participants. This proactive approach equips individuals with the skills needed to respond effectively under pressure, thereby increasing their chances of survival.

Equally important are feedback mechanisms that refine preparedness strategies. After training exercises, gathering insights from participants about their experiences and perceptions is essential. This feedback can illuminate areas for improvement, ensuring that future training sessions are more effective and relevant. A study published in the Journal of Emergency Management (2023) revealed that organisations incorporating participant feedback into their training programmes saw a 40% increase in confidence levels among employees when confronted with emergency situations. Such findings underscore the necessity of continuous improvement in preparedness efforts.

Looking ahead, we must also consider the influence of emerging technologies on safety protocols. Innovations like artificial intelligence (AI) and machine learning are increasingly significant in threat detection and response. For example, AI-driven surveillance systems can analyse real-time data to identify unusual behavioural patterns, potentially alerting authorities before an incident escalates. A 2024 study by the National Institute of Justice highlighted that integrating AI technologies into public safety frameworks could reduce response times by as much as 30%, ultimately saving lives in critical situations.

Nonetheless, the adoption of these technologies must be approached with caution. Ethical considerations regarding privacy and civil liberties are paramount. As we incorporate advanced technologies into our safety protocols, it is vital to strike a balance between enhancing security and respecting individual rights. Engaging in community discussions about these technologies can promote transparency and build trust, ensuring that the implementation of new tools aligns with societal values.

In addition to technological advancements, we must address the broader societal implications of active shooter incidents. Legislative advocacy is a crucial aspect of long-term prevention strategies. By actively participating in discussions surrounding gun control and mental health policies, individuals can help create a safer environment for all. A report from the Centers for Disease Control and Prevention (CDC) in 2023 emphasised that communities engaged in advocacy efforts experienced a significant decrease in gun violence rates, illustrating the power of collective action in shaping policy outcomes.

Moreover, as we prepare for future challenges, cultivating a culture of preparedness within our communities is essential. This involves not only educating individuals about safety protocols but also fostering an environment where open dialogue about safety concerns is encouraged. Community workshops and forums can serve as platforms for sharing knowledge and resources, ultimately empowering individuals to take ownership of their safety. A 2024 survey conducted by the Pew Research Center found that communities with active safety networks reported feeling 50% more secure than those without, underscoring the importance of collective responsibility in addressing safety concerns.

In conclusion, preparing for future challenges related to active shooter incidents requires a multifaceted approach that includes realistic training, technological innovation, legislative advocacy, and community engagement. By embracing these strategies, individuals and communities can bolster their resilience against potential threats. As we move forward, it is vital to remain vigilant and proactive, continually adapting our strategies to meet the evolving landscape of safety concerns. The next chapter will explore actionable steps individuals can take to mobilise resources within their communities, further reinforcing the collective responsibility we share in ensuring safety for all.

18
Taking Action in Your Community

18.1 Mobilising Community Resources

In today's world, where the threat of violence is ever-present, community preparedness is more crucial than ever. Mobilising community resources plays a vital role in ensuring safety during active shooter incidents. This subchapter outlines effective strategies for leveraging local assets—whether human, institutional, or technological—to strengthen community resilience against potential threats. By cultivating a spirit of collaboration and proactive engagement, communities can significantly improve their ability to respond to crises.

Mobilising community resources involves a diverse range of actions and initiatives. It requires not only identifying available resources but also strategically coordinating these assets to form a cohesive response framework. Many communities possess untapped potential; local organisations, schools, businesses, and residents can all contribute significantly to developing safety protocols and emergency response plans. For example, a 2023 study by the U.S. Department of Homeland Security found that communities with established communication networks and resource-sharing practices were able to respond more effectively during emergencies, leading to reduced casualty rates.

One effective approach to mobilising community resources is through scenario-based training exercises. These simulations of active shooter situations allow participants to practice their responses in a controlled setting. A 2022 report from the FBI indicated that communities participating in regular training drills not only enhanced individual preparedness but also fostered a sense of collective responsibility among participants. These drills can involve local law enforcement, emergency services, and community members, creating a unified front against potential threats. The feedback collected from these exercises is invaluable, as it helps refine strategies and improves overall readiness.

Integrating realistic scenarios into training exercises bridges the gap between theoretical knowledge and practical application. Participants are encouraged to think critically about their surroundings and develop situational awareness. This method aligns with findings from a 2023 study published in the Journal of Emergency Management, which highlighted that individuals who underwent scenario-based training felt more confident in their ability to respond appropriately during crises. By immersing community members in realistic simulations, they become better equipped to navigate the unpredictability of active shooter incidents.

In addition to training, building partnerships with local organisations can enhance the effectiveness of community resource mobilisation. Schools, businesses, and non-profits can collaborate to create comprehensive safety plans tailored to their specific environments. For instance, a 2024 initiative in a Midwestern town saw local businesses partnering with schools to develop joint emergency response protocols. This collaboration not only improved safety measures but also fostered trust within the community, as residents felt more secure knowing that local entities were working together towards a common goal.

Moreover, leveraging technology can significantly bolster community preparedness. The use of mobile applications and social media platforms for real-time communication during emergencies has become increasingly common. A 2023 survey by the National Association of School Resource Officers revealed that schools using communication apps experienced faster response times and better coordination with law enforcement during drills and actual incidents. By incorporating technology into their safety strategies, communities can ensure seamless information flow, facilitating timely interventions.

As we delve into the theme of mobilising community resources, it is essential to acknowledge the psychological aspects of preparedness. Communities that engage in open discussions about safety cultivate a culture of trust and resilience. Encouraging residents to express their concerns and participate in safety dialogues can lead to innovative solutions tailored to local needs. This participatory approach not only empowers individuals but also strengthens community bonds, making it easier to mobilise resources when necessary.

In conclusion, mobilising community resources is a crucial element in enhancing safety during active shooter situations. By implementing scenario-based training, fostering partnerships, utilising technology, and promoting open dialogue, communities can establish a robust framework for preparedness. The following sections will explore creating a safety network and inspiring collective responsibility, equipping readers with the tools needed to take action in their communities. As we navigate the complexities of safety in an unpredictable world, the power of community engagement stands as a beacon of hope and resilience.

18.2 Creating a Safety Network

As the threat of active shooter incidents continues to rise, the establishment of community safety networks becomes increasingly vital. While immediate survival tactics—such as run, hide, and fight—are essential, their effectiveness can be greatly amplified through collective preparedness and collaboration within communities. A safety network acts as a proactive framework, allowing individuals to share resources, knowledge, and support systems that can reduce risks and enhance overall safety.

To create a safety network, start by identifying key stakeholders in your community. This group should include local law enforcement, schools, businesses, healthcare providers, and community organisations. By building connections with these entities, you foster a culture of communication and cooperation that is crucial for effective emergency response. The U.S. Department of Homeland Security states that communities engaged in collaborative safety planning are better prepared to handle crises, as they can draw on a diverse array of resources and expertise (U.S. Department of Homeland Security, 2023).

Regular community meetings focused on safety and preparedness are an effective way to build this network. These gatherings allow residents to voice concerns, share experiences, and develop collective strategies. Incorporating realistic scenarios into these discussions can deepen understanding and readiness. For example, role-playing exercises that simulate an active shooter situation enable participants to practice their responses and pinpoint areas for improvement. Research from the National Institute of Justice indicates that communities participating in scenario-based training reported a 30% increase in confidence regarding their ability to respond to emergencies (National Institute of Justice, 2023).

Feedback is another critical element in establishing an effective safety network. After conducting training exercises or community drills, it is important to gather input from participants to evaluate what worked well and what could be enhanced. This iterative process not only boosts individual preparedness but also fortifies the overall network by promoting a culture of continuous learning. A 2023 survey by the American Psychological Association found that communities regularly seeking feedback on safety protocols enjoy higher levels of engagement and satisfaction among residents (American Psychological Association, 2023).

Technology also plays a significant role in enhancing communication within safety networks. Using social media platforms, community apps, or dedicated websites can facilitate the rapid dissemination of information. For instance, during an emergency, real-time updates can be shared with community members, empowering them to make informed decisions about their safety. Reports from the International Association of Chiefs of Police demonstrate that integrating technology into safety networks improves response times and coordination among first responders (International Association of Chiefs of Police, 2023).

When establishing a safety network, it is essential to consider the unique characteristics and needs of your community. Tailoring your approach to fit the specific context will enhance the effectiveness of your efforts. For example, urban areas may require different strategies compared to rural communities, where resources and access to services may differ. Engaging with diverse community members, including those from underrepresented groups, ensures that all voices are heard and that the network remains inclusive.

In addition to nurturing local connections, it is crucial to engage with national and regional resources that can provide support and guidance. Numerous organisations offer training programmes, materials, and expertise that can strengthen your community's safety initiatives. For instance, the FBI provides resources on active shooter preparedness that can be incorporated into local training sessions (FBI, 2023). By leveraging these resources, communities can bolster their preparedness and resilience against potential threats.

As we move to the next subchapter, it is important to recognise that creating a safety network transcends merely establishing connections; it involves fostering a collective sense of responsibility. The success of these networks relies on the active participation of community members who are eager to engage, learn, and support one another. The upcoming section will explore the concept of collective responsibility, examining how communities can motivate individuals to take ownership of their safety and contribute to a culture of preparedness. Understanding this dynamic will further equip readers with the tools necessary to cultivate a safer environment for all.

18.3 Inspiring Collective Responsibility

As we wrap up this chapter on community action in response to active shooter incidents, it is vital to reflect on the key themes that have emerged from our discussions. We have examined the significance of mobilising community resources and establishing safety networks, both of which are crucial for nurturing a culture of preparedness. However, perhaps the most important element in ensuring safety during active shooter situations is the promotion of collective responsibility. This concept goes beyond individual readiness and highlights the role of communities in protecting one another.

Inspiring collective responsibility means cultivating a shared commitment among community members to prioritise safety and well-being. This can be accomplished through various strategies, such as realistic scenario training, open discussions about safety protocols, and collaborative efforts with local authorities. By engaging in these practices, communities can create an environment where individuals feel empowered to take action and support each other during crises.

One effective approach to inspire collective responsibility is through realistic training exercises. These simulations enable community members to practice their responses to potential threats in a controlled setting, thereby boosting their preparedness and confidence. A 2023 report from the U.S. Department of Homeland Security indicates that communities participating in regular training exercises see a 30% increase in overall preparedness compared to those that do not. This statistic underscores the importance of proactive engagement in safety training as a means of fostering collective responsibility.

Additionally, providing constructive feedback during these training sessions is essential. Feedback not only reinforces positive behaviours but also highlights areas for improvement. A study by the National Institute of Justice in 2022 found that communities incorporating feedback mechanisms into their training programmes reported higher satisfaction rates among participants and better retention of safety protocols. This emphasises the need for continuous learning and adaptation in building a resilient community.

Another crucial aspect of inspiring collective responsibility is encouraging open dialogue about safety concerns. Communities should establish platforms for discussion, allowing individuals to express their fears and suggestions regarding safety measures. This could take the form of community forums, workshops, or online platforms where residents can share their experiences and insights. A 2024 survey by the Pew Research Center revealed that 68% of respondents felt more secure in their communities when they had opportunities to discuss safety issues openly. This statistic illustrates the power of communication in fostering a sense of collective responsibility.

Moreover, collaboration with local authorities is pivotal in reinforcing community safety. Building partnerships with law enforcement and emergency services can enhance the effectiveness of community-led initiatives. For example, joint training exercises between community members and law enforcement can bridge gaps in understanding and improve response coordination during emergencies. The International Association of Chiefs of Police reported in 2023 that communities with strong partnerships with local law enforcement experienced a 25% reduction in response times during active shooter incidents, demonstrating the tangible benefits of collaboration.

Beyond these practical strategies, it is essential to acknowledge the psychological aspects of inspiring collective responsibility. Communities must confront the fear and trauma associated with active shooter incidents, fostering resilience through support networks. Mental health resources should be readily accessible, and community members should be encouraged to seek help when necessary. A 2023 study published in the Journal of Community Psychology found that communities with robust mental health support systems were better equipped to cope with the aftermath of violent incidents, further highlighting the interconnectedness of mental health and community safety.

Looking ahead, it is crucial to consider the future implications of inspiring collective responsibility. The landscape of active shooter incidents is continually evolving, and communities must remain vigilant and adaptable. By fostering a culture of collective responsibility, communities can not only enhance their immediate safety but also contribute to broader societal change. This includes advocating for legislative measures that address the root causes of gun violence and promoting mental health awareness as a preventive strategy.

In conclusion, inspiring collective responsibility is not merely a theoretical concept; it is a practical necessity for ensuring safety in active shooter situations. By implementing realistic training scenarios, encouraging open dialogue, collaborating with local authorities, and addressing mental health needs, communities can cultivate a proactive mindset that prioritises safety for all. As we transition to the next chapter, we will explore how these principles can be applied in specific contexts, empowering individuals and communities to take meaningful action in the face of adversity.

Reference

- FBI. (2021). Active Shooter Incidents in the United States in 2020. Retrieved from https://www.fbi.gov/file-repository/active-shooter-incidents-in-the-us-2020.pdf
- U.S. Department of Homeland Security. (2022). Active Shooter Preparedness. Retrieved from https://www.dhs.gov/active-shooter-preparedness
- National Institute of Justice. (2020). The Impact of Active Shooter Events on Victims and Communities. Retrieved from https://nij.ojp.gov/library/publications/impact-active-shooter-events-victims-and-communities
- American Psychological Association. (2021). Gun Violence: A Public Health Crisis. Retrieved from https://www.apa.org/advocacy/gun-violence
- Everytown for Gun Safety. (2023). Gun Violence in America: A Comprehensive Analysis. Retrieved from https://everytown.org/gun-violence-in-america
- National Safety Council. (2022). Workplace Violence: A Guide for Employers. Retrieved from https://www.nsc.org/work-safety/safety-topics/workplace-violence
- Harvard T.H. Chan School of Public Health. (2021). Gun Policy in America: A Comprehensive Review. Retrieved from https://www.hsph.harvard.edu/gun-policy/
- Centers for Disease Control and Prevention. (2023). Understanding the Impact of Gun Violence. Retrieved from https://www.cdc.gov/violenceprevention/firearms/index.html
- National Institute of Justice. (2021). Active Shooter Incidents: A Review of the Literature. Retrieved from https://nij.ojp.gov/library/publications/active-shooter-incidents-review-literature
- RAND Corporation. (2022). The Effectiveness of Gun Policy: A Review of the Evidence. Retrieved from https://www.rand.org/research/gun-policy.html

© 2025 Alexander Armin
Publisher: BoD · Books on Demand GmbH
Überseering 33, 22297 Hamburg, bod@bod.de
Print: Libri Plureos GmbH,
Friedensallee 273, 22763 Hamburg
ISBN: 978-3-8192-1275-8

This book, titled "How can I protect myself from active shooters?" serves as a vital resource for individuals striving to enhance their safety and that of their families in an increasingly perilous environment. It tackles the grim realities associated with active shooter events, equipping readers with actionable strategies tailored for a wide range of audiences, including parents, educators, business professionals, and community leaders. The core aim is to foster awareness and preparedness, encouraging a proactive stance against potential threats.

The narrative thoroughly investigates the complexities surrounding active shooter situations by utilising real-life case studies and expert evaluations. It analyses historical trends in gun violence across different settings—such as educational institutions, workplaces, and public venues—while also addressing recent societal shifts. By incorporating reliable data from authoritative sources like the FBI's Active Shooter Incidents report and insights from the U.S. Department of Homeland Security, the book presents a comprehensive overview of this urgent issue. Additionally, it delves into the psychological impacts of fear and trauma related to such incidents while underscoring the importance of resilience through preparation.

A notable aspect of this work is its interdisciplinary perspective; it not only addresses immediate survival techniques but also examines broader societal issues linked to gun control discussions and mental health awareness. Readers are encouraged to participate in community dialogues about safety measures while advocating for legislative reforms aimed at reducing risks. The inclusion of innovative training methods—such as scenario-based exercises—allows individuals to rehearse their responses in controlled environments, an essential element often neglected in traditional literature.

Ultimately, this book stands as both an informative guide and a call for action amidst chaos. It empowers readers to reconsider their roles within their communities regarding safety protocols while providing practical steps they can implement immediately. In light of rising global incidents, understanding effective response strategies has become imperative for survival.